The Heart Attack Sūtra

The Heart Attack Sūtra

A New Commentary on the Heart Sūtra

by Karl Brunnhölzl

SNOW LION
BOSTON & LONDON

Snow Lion
An imprint of Shambhala Publications, Inc.
Horticultural Hall
300 Massachusetts Avenue
Boston, Massachusetts 02115
www.shambhala.com

9 8 7 6 5 4 3 2

Printed in the United States of America

⊗ This edition is printed on acid-free paper that meets the American
National Standards Institute Z39.48 Standard.
♻ Shambhala Publications makes every effort to print on recycled paper.
For more information please visit www.shambhala.com.

Distributed in the United States by Random House, Inc., and in Canada by
Random House of Canada Ltd

Library of Congress Cataloging-in-Publication Data
Brunnhölzl, Karl.
The heart attack sūtra: a new commentary on the Heart Sūtra / by Karl
Brunnhölzl.
p. cm.
Includes bibliographical references.
ISBN 978-1-55939-391-1 (alk. paper)
1. Tripiṭaka. Sūtrapiṭaka. Prajñāpāramitā. Hṛdaya—Commentaries. I. Title.
BQ1967.B77 2012
294.3'85—dc23
2011040532

Contents

Introduction

THE CRAZINESS OF THE *HEART SŪTRA*

There is no doubt that the *Heart Sūtra* is the most frequently used and recited text in the entire mahāyāna Buddhist tradition, which still flourishes in Japan, Korea, Vietnam, Tibet, Mongolia, Bhutan, China, parts of India and Nepal, and, more recently, also in the Americas and Europe. Many people have said many different things about what the *Heart Sūtra* is and what it is not, such as being the heart of wisdom, a statement of how things truly are, the key teaching of the mahāyāna, a condensation of all the prajñāpāramitā sūtras (the Buddha's second turning of the wheel of dharma), or an explanation of emptiness in a nutshell. Before we get to the actual words of the *Heart Sūtra*, it might be helpful to first explore a little bit of its background within the Buddhist tradition as well as the meanings of "prajñāpāramitā" and "emptiness."

In brief, what we can safely say about the *Heart Sūtra* is that it is completely crazy. If we read it, it does not make any sense. Well, maybe the beginning and end make sense, but everything in the middle sounds like a sophisticated form of nonsense, which can be said to be the basic feature of the prajñāpāramitā sūtras in general. If we like the word "no," we might like the sūtra because that is the main word it uses—no this, no that, no everything. We could also say that it is a sūtra about wisdom, but it is a sūtra about crazy wisdom. When we read it, it sounds nuts, but that is actually where the wisdom part comes in. What the *Heart Sūtra* (like all prajñāpāramitā sūtras) does is to cut through, deconstruct, and demolish all our usual conceptual frameworks, all our rigid ideas, all our belief systems, all our reference points, including any with regard to our spiritual path. It does so on a very fundamental level, not just in terms of thinking and concepts, but also in terms of our perception, how we see the world, how we hear, how we smell, taste, touch, how we regard and emotionally react to ourselves and others, and so on. This sūtra pulls the rug out from underneath our feet and does not leave anything intact that we can think of, nor even a lot of things that we cannot even think of. This is called "crazy wisdom." I guess I should give you a warning here that this sūtra is hazardous to your saṃsāric sanity. What Sangharakshita says about the *Diamond Sūtra* equally applies to all prajñāpāramitā sūtras, including the *Heart Sūtra*:

> . . . if we insist that the requirements of the logical mind be satisfied, we are missing the point. What the *Diamond Sūtra* is actually delivering is not a systematic treatise, but a series of sledgehammer blows, attacking from this side and that, to try and break through our fundamental delusion. It is not going to make things easy for the logical mind by putting things in a logical form. This sūtra is going to be confusing, irritating, annoying, and unsatisfying—and perhaps we cannot ask for it to be otherwise. If it were all set forth neatly and clearly, leaving no loose ends, we might be in danger of thinking we had grasped the Perfection of Wisdom.[1]

Another way to look at the *Heart Sūtra* is that it represents a very condensed contemplation manual. It is not just something to be read or recited, but the intention is to contemplate on its meaning in as detailed a way as possible. Since it is the *Heart Sūtra*, it conveys the heart essence of what is called *prajñāpāramitā*, the "perfection of wisdom or insight." In itself, it does not fuss around, or give us all the details. It is more like a brief memo for contemplating all the elements of our psychophysical existence from the point of view of what we are now, what we become as we progress on the Buddhist path, and what we attain (or do not attain) at the end of that path. If we want to read all the details, we have to go

---

1   Sangharakshita 1993, p. 44.

to the longer prajñāpāramitā sūtras, which make up about twenty-one thousand pages in the Tibetan Buddhist canon—twenty-one thousand pages of "no." The longest sūtra alone, in one hundred thousand lines, consists of twelve large books. The *Heart Sūtra* is on the lower end, so to speak, and the shortest sūtra consists of just one letter, which is my personal favorite. It starts with the usual introduction, "Once the Buddha was dwelling in Rājagṛha at Vulture Flock Mountain" and so on, and then he said, "A." It ends with all the gods and so on rejoicing, and that's it. It is said that there are people who actually realize the meaning of the prajñāpāramitā sūtras through just hearing or reading "A."

Besides being a meditation manual, we could also say that the *Heart Sūtra* is like a big koan. But it is not just *one* koan, it is like those Russian dolls: there is one big doll on the outside and then there is a smaller one inside that first one, and there are many more smaller ones in each following one. Likewise, all the "no's" in the big koan of the sūtra are little koans. Every little phrase with a "no" is a different koan in terms of what the "no" relates to, such as "no eye," "no ear," and so on. It is an invitation to contemplate what that means. "No eye," "no ear" sounds very simple and very straightforward, but if we go into the details, it is not that straightforward at all. In other words, all those different "no"-phrases give us different angles or facets of the main theme of the sūtra, which is emptiness. Emptiness means that things do not exist as they seem, but are like illusions and like dreams. They do not have a nature or a findable core of their own. Each one of those phrases makes us look at that very same message. The message or the looking are not really different, but we look at it in relation to different things. What does it mean that the eye is empty? What does it mean that visible form is empty? What does it mean that even wisdom, buddhahood, and nirvāṇa are empty?

From an ordinary Buddhist point of view we could even say that the *Heart Sūtra* is not only crazy, but it is iconoclastic or even heretical. Many people have complained about the prajñāpāramitā sūtras because they also trash all the hallmarks of Buddhism itself, such as the four noble truths, the Buddhist path, and nirvāṇa. These sūtras not only say that our ordinary thoughts, emotions, and perceptions are invalid and that they do not really exist as they seem to, but that the same goes for all the concepts and frameworks of philosophical schools—non-Buddhist schools, Buddhist schools, and even the mahāyāna, the tradition to which the prajñāpāramitā sūtras belong. Is there any other spiritual tradition that says, "Everything that we teach, just forget about it"? It is somewhat similar to the boss of Microsoft recently having publicly recommended that PC users should not buy Windows Vista anymore, but instead go straight from Windows XP to Windows 7. Basically, he was advertising against his own product. The *Heart Sūtra* is similar to that, except that it tells us only what not to buy, but not what to buy instead.

In brief, if we have never seen the *Heart Sūtra* and we read it, it sounds crazy because it just keeps saying "no, no, no." If we are trained in Buddhism, it also sounds crazy (maybe even more so) because it negates everything that we have learned and try to cultivate.

Why is it called the *"Heart Sūtra"*? It has that name because it teaches the heart of the mahāyāna, primarily in terms of the view. However, the basic motivation of the mahāyāna is also implicitly contained in this sūtra in the form of Avalokiteśvara, the great bodhisattva who is the embodiment of the loving-kindness and compassion of all buddhas. It is actually the only prajñāpāramitā sūtra in which Avalokiteśvara appears at all, and in it he is even the main speaker. Thus, the *Heart Sūtra* teaches emptiness through the epitome of compassion. It is often said that, in a sense, emptiness is the heart of the mahāyāna, but the heart of emptiness is compassion. The scriptures even use the phrase "emptiness with a heart of compassion." It is crucial to never forget that. The main reason for Avalokiteśvara's presence here is to symbolize the aspect of compassion and to emphasize that we should not miss out on it. If we just read all the "no's" and then get hooked on the "no path" of "no self" and "no attainment," it gets a little dreary or depressing and we may wonder, "Why are we doing this?" or "Why are we not doing this?" In fact, the heart essence of the prajñāpāramitā teachings and the mahāyāna is the union of emptiness and compassion. If we look at the larger prajñāpāramitā sūtras, we see that they teach both aspects extensively. In addition to teaching about emptiness, they also speak about the path in great detail, such as how to cultivate loving-kindness and compassion, how to do certain meditations, and how to progress through the paths. They do not always say "no," but also sometimes present things in a more positive light. Even the *Heart Sūtra*, towards the end, comes up with a few phrases without "no."

Without developing a soft heart and compassion, which like water softens our mental rigidity, there is a danger that the teachings on emptiness can make our hearts even harder. If we think we understand emptiness, but our compassion does not increase, or even lessens, we are on the wrong track. Therefore, for those of us who are Buddhists, it is good and necessary to give rise to compassion and bodhicitta before we study, recite, and contemplate this sūtra. All others may connect with any spot of compassion that they can find in their hearts.

In yet another way, we could say that the *Heart Sūtra* is an invitation to just let go and relax. We can replace all the words in this sūtra that go with "no," such as "no eye," "no ear," with all our problems, such as "no depression," "no fear," "no unemployment," "no war," and so on. That might sound simplistic, but if we do that and actually make it into a contemplation on what all those things such as depression, fear, war, and economic crisis actually are, it can become very powerful, maybe even more powerful than the original words in the sūtra. Usually we are not that interested in, for example, our ears and whether they really exist or not, so with regard to contemplating what emptiness means, one of the basic principles of the prajñāpāramitā sūtras is to make the examination as personal as possible. It is not about reciting some stereotypical formula or the *Heart Sūtra* without ever getting to the core of our own clinging to real existence with regard to those phenomena to which we obviously do cling, or our own ego-clinging. For example, the *Heart Sūtra* does not say "no self," "no home," "no partner," "no job," "no money," which are the things we usually care about. Therefore, in order to make it more relevant to our life, we have to fill those in. The *Heart Sūtra* gives us a basic template of how to contemplate emptiness, but the larger prajñāpāramitā sūtras fill in a lot of stuff, not only saying "no eye," "no ear," and so on. They go through endless lists of all kinds of phenomena, so we are welcome to come up with our own personal lists of phenomena that map out our personal universe and then apply the approach of the *Heart Sūtra* to those lists.

There are accounts in several of the larger prajñāpāramitā sūtras about people being present in the audience who had already attained certain advanced levels of spiritual development or insight that liberated them from saṃsāric existence and suffering. These people, who are called "arhats" in Buddhism, were listening to the Buddha speaking about emptiness and then had different reactions. Some thought, "This is crazy, let's go" and left. Others stayed, but some of them had heart attacks, vomited blood, and died. It seems they didn't leave in time. These arhats were so shocked by what they were hearing that they died on the spot. That's why somebody suggested recently that we could call the *Heart Sūtra* the *Heart Attack Sūtra*. Another meaning of that could be that this sūtra goes right for the heart of the matter, while mercilessly attacking all ego trips that prevent us from waking up to our true heart. In any case, so far nobody has had a heart attack here, which is good news. But the bad news is that probably nobody understood it either.

EMPTINESS MEANS LETTING GO
Grounded in Groundlessness

The *Heart Sūtra* and the other prajñāpāramitā sūtras talk about a lot of things, but their most fundamental theme is the basic groundlessness of our experience. They say that no matter what we do, no matter what we say, and no matter what we feel, we need not believe any of it. There is nothing whatsoever to hold on to, and even that is not sure. So these sūtras pull the rug out from under us all the time and take away all our favorite toys. Usually, when someone takes away one of our mental toys, we just find new toys. That is one of the reasons why many of the prajñāpāramitā sūtras are so long—they list all the toys we can think of and even more, but our mind still keeps grasping at new ones. The basic point is to get to a place where we actually stop searching for and grasping at the next toy. Then we need to see how *that* state of mind feels. How does our mind feel when we are not grasping at anything, when we are not trying to entertain ourselves, and when our mind is not going outside (or not going anywhere at all), when there is no place left to go?

When we are at sea far away from any land and we let a land-dwelling bird fly from our ship, the bird does not get very far. Eventually it will always come back to the ship because it is the only place for it to land. In the same way, our thoughts and emotions always try to go somewhere or fly into the sky of exciting things, but they cannot really go anywhere outside of our mind, and eventually they will always settle back into the very mind in which they arose. Therefore, we do not have to nail down our thoughts, it is okay if they move. Even if they move far away, we do not have to worry about them, run after them, or send off a search party. Inevitably, they will always settle into the mind, so we never lose any thoughts. That means we do not have to chase them or bring them back. Fundamentally, we can never get out of our mind, though sometimes we feel that we are out of our mind. But we can never step out of our mind and see what the world is like from outside of our mind. The prajñāpāramitā sūtras talk about this fundamental experience of coming back to our mind just as it is, without going anywhere, without doing anything, without manipulating anything, just letting our mind be as it is. We usually do not do that, but instead always try to make our mind do something.

Therefore, emptiness is about the nowness of all phenomena, being in the present moment without any sense of solid or lasting things, the sheer experience of the mind's infinite display without anything to pin-point or hold on to.

When we look at the meaning of emptiness (and we will look at it in more detail below), the Sanskrit word is *śūnyatā*. One of the literal meanings of *śūnya* is "empty" and another one is "zero." In Indian mathematics, the zero sign is *śūnya*, but it has quite a different meaning from "zero" in the West. When we think of zero, we think "nothing," but in India the circle of *śūnya*, or zero, means "fullness," "complete-ness," or "wholeness." In the same way, "emptiness" does not mean "nothingness," but rather "fullness" in the sense of full potential—anything can happen in emptiness and because of emptiness. A lot of people think that if nothing really exists, how can anything function? However, Nāgārjuna said that it is precisely because everything does not really exist that everything functions. If everything were truly existent, existing in and of itself and thus being unchanging, things would not depend on anything. But then they could not interact with each other either because that entails change. Therefore, it is only due to everything changing all the time that interaction and functioning are possible.

The root of the word *śūnya* means "to swell," which implies the notion of hollowness. In this way, the phenomena of seeming reality outwardly appear to be real and solid, while actually resembling empty balloons which are only inflated by our ignorance. Through our ignorance we inflate a lot of nothings into very big somethings. When they swell up, that is the circle, or balloon, of *śūnya*. Thus, *śūnyatā* is not just nothingness, but everything coming out of the infinite space of phenomena in which nothing can be pinpointed but everything can happen. In this sense *śūnyatā* means the complete potential for everything to arise and it also means dependent origination. Everything that seems to be real is just like blown-up balloons—a lot of hot air and not much else, if anything. This is also what the etymology of "to swell" for *śūnya* points to. As long as it is unquestioned, our seeming reality seems to be "swell," but when we reflect and meditate on emptiness, all those balloons that we usually entertain ourselves with become punctured and are revealed as what they really are, which is just the hot air within them.

When we look at the concept of zero in mathematics, if we just take one zero, it seems to be nothing, but many zeros following any other number mean a lot, such as "one hundred," "one thousand," or "one billion." This shows that infinite quantities can come from zero. Therefore, it is not just nothing. Likewise, emptiness is not "nothing," which is emphasized in many Buddhist texts over and over again. However, it is not "something" either. Usually we think that if a given phenomenon is not something, it must be nothing, and if it is not nothing, it must be something. But emptiness is just a word for pointing out the fact that no matter what we say or think about something, it does not really correctly characterize that something because our dualistic mind just gets stuck in one extreme or the other. Thus, we could say that emptiness is like thinking outside of the box, that is, the box of black-and-white thinking or dualistic thinking. As long as we stay within the ballpark of dualistic thinking, there is always existence, nonexistence, permanence, extinction, good, and bad. Within that frame of reference, we will never get beyond it, no matter if we are religious, a scientist, a Buddhist, an agnostic, or whatever. Emptiness tells us that we have to step out of that ballpark altogether. Emptiness points to the most radical transformation of our entire outlook with regard to ourselves and the world. Emptiness not only means the end of the world as we know it, but that this world never really existed in the first place. If we really understand what that means, it is so scary we may freak out or have heart attacks like those arhats. Not necessarily, of course, because there are also reports of people who actually got it and had no heart attacks. Nevertheless, the main point is to dare to step into the infinite space of groundlessness, which is frightening because it questions everything that we are and everything that we think.

Emptiness, Dependent Origination, and Quantum Physics

In a sense, the teachings on emptiness have a lot of parallels with quantum physics. Quantum physicists tell us that there is really no world out there, nor a body. There is actually not much, if anything. They are still looking for *something*, because it sounds better and we do not have to be scared that there is really nothing at all to hold on to. When physicists talk about a quantum field, it almost entirely consists of space and some energy in it, not even particles. They may talk about "particles," but this term does not refer to any kind of substance anymore, just statistical probabilities of relationships. This is also very much what emptiness is about, meaning that there is no single phenomenon whatsoever that exists independently on its own. The description of a quantum field is very much like the *Heart Sūtra's* formula "Form is emptiness. Emptiness is form. Emptiness is nothing other than form, and form is nothing other than emptiness." Everything is interrelated and constantly changing in every moment, yet entirely ungraspable.

In quantum physics, they have found that if one electron or one subtle particle on one end of the universe changes, another one at the other end of the universe also changes. Thus, it is not that this principle of interdependence is limited to a certain domain or area in space; it is truly infinite and all-pervasive. The Buddha said the same—dependent origination is an infinite web of causes and conditions. However, "causes and conditions" does not refer to little things that spin around each other and do stuff because if we take a close look, none of them can really be found. If we do not analyze all those causes, conditions, and their results, everything seems to work fine (at least most of the time). But when we take a deeper look into how things actually work or what things actually are, it gets very fuzzy. This same phenomenon is found in quantum physics too—the more the physicists look and the more subtle particles they find, the smaller and smaller and more elusive these particles become until they cannot even call them "particles" anymore. They just apply names and schemata to an ongoing process, which sort of freezes this inconceivable and constantly changing process into something a little bit more tangible, such as mathematical equations or formulas. Similarly, when the Buddha spoke from the perspective of emptiness, he was doing so in a way similar to physicists talking about quantum mechanics, using the formula "Form is emptiness; emptiness also is form." Fundamentally, we can never really describe exactly what is happening. We can observe the process in the lab and say, "Wow!" and that's about it. Later, we try to express what happened, the same way the Buddha did when he described to his students how things are from the perspective of his awakening into true reality.

THE BUDDHA'S THREE CYCLES OF TEACHING
Expressing the Inexpressible

Buddha's enlightenment was like that "Wow!" moment in a lab, and at first he did not want to speak about it to anybody. According to the *Lalitavistarasūtra*, he uttered this spontaneous verse:

> I have found a nectarlike dharma,
> Profound, peaceful, free from reference points, luminous,
>   and unconditioned.
> Whoever I would teach it to could not understand it.
> Thus, I shall just stay silent in the middle of the forest.[2]

---

2   XXV.1.

And that is what he did for quite a while, obviously thinking that nobody would understand what his realization of mind's true nature is. However, later he was encouraged by others to teach, and then he did nothing but that for the remaining forty-five years of his life. This may seem very strange—how can he teach for forty-five years about something that nobody will understand anyway? As the Buddha said, his realization of the nature of the mind is indeed inexpressible and inconceivable, but that does not mean that it is completely inaccessible, which is a big difference. It is inconceivable, but there still is a path that leads us to eventually experiencing that very same realization. It is still inconceivable, but our experience of it is also inconceivable. Possessing this insight as well as the infinite compassion and capacity to actually show others how to reach mental freedom, the Buddha taught what cannot be taught. Obviously we cannot experience the taste of delicious food simply by talking or hearing about it. Still, we might become inspired to create delicious food in order to experience its taste. In the same way, we might become inspired to make some effort to experience the taste of enlightenment while not mistaking the words for their referents.

The Buddha realized that there are ways to communicate his awakening. All of them are indirect instructions, but if others work with these instructions in their minds, they can actually realize what the Buddha had realized. As the Indian Buddhist poet Aśvaghoṣa said:

> We use words to become free from words
> Until we reach the pure wordless essence.

In this way, the Buddhist teachings are like fingers pointing to the moon. The problem is that if we get stuck on the fingers we will never see the moon. The Buddha provided a lot of pointing fingers for forty-five years, always pointing to that same moon, which is nothing other than the true nature of our mind. The reason why he used so many pointing fingers is that if a single person points to the moon with just one finger, we might miss it. But if many people point at the moon with many fingers from all kinds of directions, it is harder to miss the moon. This is why the Buddha gave so many different teachings, all like fingers pointing from different directions. Of course, since they are pointing from different directions, a lot of people said, "This is exactly the opposite of what he said the other day." True, but he was just pointing at the very same moon from another direction. It is like asking two people for directions to the White House, with one of them standing to its left and the other standing to its right. The first person will point to the right and the second to the left. If we think that one of them must be wrong or that they contradict each other, we obviously miss the point (and the White House).

To give a little bit more context to what happened in the Buddha's teaching career before he taught the *Heart Sūtra*, in the mahāyāna tradition it is said that the Buddha taught three cycles of teachings, called "dharma wheels." This is a division in terms of their contents, not in terms of their sequence in time. The Buddha started out by talking about the basic human condition, also known as the four noble truths. He began by teaching about what we like most—suffering. Then he spoke about the causes of suffering, or the origin of suffering. Next he said that we can actually stop all our suffering and its causes, which is the third truth, of the cessation of suffering. The fourth noble truth is the path, the methods for accomplishing the end of suffering. Thus, the Buddha did not talk about emptiness initially, he did not teach the prajñāpāramitā sūtras in the beginning. It is pretty obvious why not— there would have been no Buddhism. If he had taught something like the *Heart Sūtra* right away, people would just have said, "Are you crazy?" and left. Instead, the Buddha was trying to prepare the ground for more profound insights, such as emptiness, by teaching the four noble truths. This means he first taught people about our basic situation. To a lesser or greater degree, suffering is common to everybody, but most people try to ignore their suffering or brush it away. In addition, they are ignorant about the causes of suffering, that it can be ended for good, and that there are the means to end it. This is what the Buddha taught first at the Deer Park in Sarnath in India. His first teaching was to only five people, his companions in ascetic practices before he sat under the bodhi tree and attained buddhahood. It is said that these first five students of the Buddha attained liberation from saṃsāra (arhathood) merely through hearing his teaching on the four noble truths.

The second cycle of the Buddha's teachings is the one to which the *Heart Sūtra* belongs. This cycle consists of the prajñāpāramitā teachings and is called "the dharma wheel of no characteristics." This set of teachings was given on a mountain in India called "Vulture Flock Mountain," which is near Rājagṛha in present-day Bihar. At the time of the Buddha, this town was the seat of a very powerful king, who was a friend and sponsor of the Buddha. When Buddha Śākyamuni taught the second cycle of his teachings, there was a huge audience; the sūtras speak of thousands of monks and thousands of bodhisattvas as well as many nonhuman beings, such as gods and other aliens.

If you ever get a chance to go to Vulture Flock Mountain, it is worth the trip. If there is any place in the world where you can get a glimpse of emptiness just through being there, this is the place to go. Of course, this is just my projection, but I found it very impressive and I did not really want to leave; there was a sense of having stepped out of time and space.

Anyway, in that second cycle of teachings the Buddha taught mainly about *śūnyatā*, that nothing is what it seems. At the same time, he also taught about compassion because he said that beings suffer due to their clinging to things as existing in the way they appear. They cling to castles in the sky which can never fulfill their desire for happiness. So they need to wake up and see what is actually there, and how to pursue happiness in a more promising way. This is where compassion comes in, because if someone like the Buddha realizes how things actually are and that beings suffer only because they hold on to nonexistent delusive appearances, that person naturally wants to point out that such suffering is solely based on misperception and is completely unnecessary. Ultimately speaking, saṃsāric suffering is just an error, like a bug in a software program—it should not happen, but it does. This is why the Buddha taught for forty-five years. Though he realized that he could not really communicate what he experienced, he could not bear seeing all these beings immersed in suffering, which from the perspective of how things actually are, is completely unnecessary and can be removed. Therefore, the two main things that the Buddha taught in the second cycle are emptiness and compassion.

In the third cycle he also taught about emptiness and compassion, but in addition he spoke about what is called "buddha nature." In a sense, if understood correctly, this is not really something different from emptiness, but refers more to the subjective side of actually experiencing or living emptiness as opposed to emptiness as a mere object or fact. In other words, buddha nature speaks about the emptiness of our own mind—the nature of our own mind, which is emptiness, and at the same time is clarity, luminosity, awareness, and wakefulness. Also, the third cycle distinguishes between what is of expedient meaning and of definitive meaning in all the teachings of the Buddha. In this way, the third cycle clarifies all the finger-pointings, so to speak, such as whether a certain finger points this way or that way in order not to confuse them or to see them as contradictory.

The Teachings as Scriptures and Realization

The general definition of a "dharma wheel" is "the teachings of the Buddha, consisting of both scriptures and realization, which eliminate the factors in the mind streams of the beings to be guided that obscure liberation from saṃsāra and a buddha's omniscience." Thus, such a dharma wheel, or cycle of teaching, is presented as being twofold—the dharma of realization and the dharma of scriptures. Among these, the dharma of realization is defined as "the reality of the purified phenomena that are produced by having become familiar with the mind that thoroughly discriminates phenomena." This consists of the cessation of suffering and the path that leads to it. Thus, the dharma of realization is the real deal—it refers to our mind actually becoming the mind of a buddha via being taught through the scriptures, oral teachings, video dharma, or nonverbal symbols. Therefore, the more important dharma is the dharma of realization, which means to experience or be the same as what the Buddha experienced.

Interestingly, the nature of the dharma wheel of the scriptures is defined as "the mind of a disciple that appears either in the form of a buddha's speech (whose main topics are either the causes, the results, or the nature of nirvāṇa) or that mind which appears as the collections of names, words, and letters that serve as the support for such speech." Of course, this is a definition very much from the point of view of emptiness or the relative and subjective nature of all things. It does not say that there are any real material texts or teachings out there, any external buddhas to teach us, or any material sounds coming into our ears. Basically, like everything else, the teaching situation happens nowhere other than in our own mind. It is our own mind that takes on the form of the texts, sounds, buddhas, and their teachings that appear to us. However, it does not do so randomly by itself, but under the guiding influence of a buddha's wisdom mind. In other words, in dependence on the dominant condition that is a buddha's omniscient wisdom and the causal condition that consists of the relatively pure mind streams of certain beings to be guided, the wheel of dharma of the scriptures is nothing but the very mind of these beings appearing for them in the form of words and letters. Since buddhas neither have any latent tendencies that would give rise to some speech of theirs nor possess any ignorance of clinging to inner mind as being external sounds, ultimately such a dharma wheel is not a teaching that results from any wish of a buddha to teach.

Thus, on the most fundamental level, when a buddha teaches the dharma, it is a direct mind-to-mind exchange. Of course, for most people it does not appear that way because it is inaccessible for our ordinary senses and our conceptual mind. Ordinary beings like us always have to rely on some form, some concept, or something to hold on to. We cannot directly perceive the mind of a buddha, otherwise we would be buddhas too. Therefore, we need some mirror or we need some "sideways" communication. We could say that the mind of a buddha is mirrored in our own mind, not directly, but in the form of texts, teachings, teachers, and so on. This is what serves as the remedy for our problems and their causes, such as our wrong ideas, our weird emotions, and the ensuing unskillful actions.

This presentation of the dharma wheel of scriptures shows why it is often said that from the Buddha's own perspective he actually never taught a single word. The sūtras say that the Buddha, from the moment when he attained enlightenment to the moment when he passed into nirvāṇa, did not speak a single word. At the same time, the texts say that this not-speaking satisfied the needs of all beings as a continuous rain of dharma. For the Buddha's mind is reflected in the minds of other beings, and through that interaction certain things happen in the minds of those beings, which can appear as texts, as teachings, or as all kinds of other things that serve as instructions about their minds. Nāgārjuna's *Ratnāvalī* says:

> Just as a grammarian
> Initially teaches the alphabet,
> The Buddha teaches the dharma
> Just as those to be guided can absorb it.
>
> To some, he teaches the dharma
> In order to turn them away from evil;
> To some, so that they accomplish merit;
> To some, what is based on duality;
>
> To some, what is based on nonduality;
> To some, what is profound and frightening to the fearful;
> And to some, the means for enlightenment
> That is emptiness with a heart of compassion.[3]

Here we can see the whole range of the Buddhist teachings. Different beings were taught very different things. All of these teachings are like fingers pointing to the moon, but some fingers point more directly and others more indirectly, and the manner of pointing also depends on the capacities of those beings.

PRAJÑĀPĀRAMITĀ—PERFECT WISDOM GONE BEYOND

Like all prajñāpāramitā sūtras, the *Heart Sūtra* belongs to the second cycle of the Buddha's teachings, the teachings on emptiness (or prajñāpāramitā), also called "the dharma wheel of the lack of characteristics." As the *Heart Sūtra* says:

---

3 IV.94–96.

Thus, Śāriputra, all phenomena are emptiness, without characteristics . . .

So what is prajñāpāramitā? Basically it means "perfection of wisdom" or "perfection of insight." The sūtras never say "perfection of emptiness" or "perfection of the nature of phenomena." In terms of subject and object, emptiness, or the nature of phenomena, is more on the object side as what is to be realized. Of course, there is nothing to be perfected in emptiness, or the nature of phenomena anyway; it is naturally perfect in itself. However, there is a lot to be perfected in our understanding and realization of emptiness or the nature of phenomena, our insight into how things truly are. This insight is called *prajñā*, which means to see how things actually are through finely and thoroughly discriminating them. When that insight has reached its highest point, it is called *prajñāpāramitā*, "the perfection of prajñā." Thus, prajñāpāramitā refers both to the fruition or the outcome—the full perfection of that insight—and also to the process of arriving at such perfection. When we speak about prajñāpāramitā, we are talking about our mind and its basic capacity to realize how things actually are beyond superficial appearances. How we arrive at this realization is through training this prajñā, which is not something that we need to reinvent or import from somewhere. It is present in everybody's mind and just needs to be developed to its fullest bloom. Buddhahood means having developed the basic potential of every sentient being to its complete maturation.

Prajñā does not refer to passive knowledge, such as knowing facts from the *Guinness Book of Records* or knowing how to get from Seattle to New York. Rather, prajñā is the active inquisitiveness of our mind, its basic curiosity of wanting to know and wanting to find out how things really are. That is the essence of prajñā. If we look at the Buddha's own career, this is exactly how he started. He did not start with the answers or by following some religion, tradition, or code of behavior. He started with questions. As Prince Siddhārtha he lived in his sheltered existence in the palace of his parents, who wished to protect him from the bad world (as all parents do). However, eventually he got out with his charioteer and saw things he had never seen before, such as an old person.

He pointed at him and asked his charioteer, "What is that?" The charioteer answered, "This is an old person." Siddhārtha continued, "Does this happen to everyone?" "Yes, even to you." The same exchange took place when Siddhārtha saw a dying person and a sick person. The next time he saw a meditator under a tree and the charioteer explained, "This guy tries to overcome all the problems that you saw before." Every time Siddhārtha realized, "I do not really know what is going on here" and he tried to find out.

This is the hallmark of the Buddhist path—trying to find out what is really going on in every moment, what is going on in our mind, what is going on in our environment, and what is going on with other people. In this way, prajñā entails basic intelligence, intelligence in its original meaning, which is deep insight and the ability to finely discriminate and distinguish things. From a Buddhist point of view there are different levels of prajñā—mundane prajñā and supramundane prajñā. The first one is any form of insight or wisdom that has nothing to do with the Buddhist path, such as learning things in school or being a scientist. Supramundane prajñā is the primary mental factor that is the driving force, or motor, on the Buddhist path. It is said that prajñā is the very essence of the Buddhist path because this path is about realizing how things really are. Thus, prajñāpāramitā is the highest form of supramundane prajñā because it is the most supreme of all prajñās, focuses on ultimate reality, and makes us proceed to the great nirvāṇa of not abiding in either saṃsāra or the limited nirvāṇa of personal liberation and peace. In other words, it dissolves all our ordinary reference points and rigid ideas, making us transcend the world as we know it, with all its problems and suffering.

Another meaning of prajñāpāramitā is "transcendent insight." What are we transcending? We transcend all our ordinary hang-ups and problems, which are also known as saṃsāra. Where are we going? As usual in Buddhism, different people give different answers. Some people say we are not going anywhere because there is nothing to go to. To go anywhere would mean to go outside of our mind. In fact, the Buddhist path is not really about going anywhere. Though "path" sounds as if we start somewhere and then end up somewhere else, while we keep walking in between, "path" in Buddhism is a synonym for "mind." The path refers to the mental process of developing our basic human potential to its fullest. Therefore, the path is something that happens on the inside, not on the outside. Whether we are on the Buddhist path or not is not so much determined by what we say and what we do, but mainly by what is going on in our mind.

Prajñāpāramitā can also be understood as "having gone beyond" or "having gone to the other shore." Traditionally, it is said that we are constantly drowning in the big ocean of saṃsāra with all its many kinds of suffering. The other shore, when we have crossed this ocean, is called "nirvāṇa." This is one explanation, which is obviously still very dualistic, saying, "First, we are at one place, then we have to cross this ocean, and finally we are somewhere else." Therefore, this is just a provisional description. A more subtle way to understand this is that "gone beyond" does not really mean to go anywhere, but to have a complete change of outlook. We remain in exactly the same "place," if there is any, but we altogether change our outlook of what happens in that place and also of that place itself. Buddhism often speaks about pure lands, or buddha realms, but they do not really exist somewhere outside, they are in our mind. It depends on our state of mind whether we are in a buddha realm or not. We all have glimpses of that, once in a while, when we are in a really good mood and everything seems to be wonderful and completely flawless, which is like a buddha realm. But when we are in a really bad mood, even if the sun is shining and everybody is nice to us, we still feel like a being in hell.

The Flaming Sword of Prajñā—Sharp, Illuminating, and Compassionate Inquisitiveness

As the basic inquisitiveness and curiosity of our mind, prajñā is both precise and playful at the same time. Iconographically it is often depicted as a double-bladed, flaming sword which is extremely sharp. Such a sword obviously needs to be handled with great care, and may even seem somewhat threatening. Prajñā is indeed threatening to our ego and to our cherished belief systems since it undermines our very notion of reality and the reference points upon which we build our world. Prajñā questions who we are and what we perceive. Since this sword cuts both ways, it not only serves to slice up our very solid-looking objective reality, but it also cuts through the subjective experiencer of such a reality. In this way, it is also that which makes us see through our own ego trips and self-inflation. It takes some effort to continuously fool ourselves about ourselves. Prajñā means being found out by ourselves, which first of all requires taking an honest look at the games we play.

Therefore, prajñā becomes even more important as we progress along the path because our ego trips just become more sophisticated. First, when we are not spiritual, our ego just thinks, "I'm pretty good." But then, when we become spiritual, our ego thinks, "Now I'm also spiritual! Now I'm on the path! Now I'm a Buddhist! Now I can realize emptiness and develop great compassion and all those buddha qualities!" Obviously something needs to be done about that, which is the job of prajñā. It has this self-checking quality. Whenever we go off the track and whenever the balloon of our ego-inflation becomes too big, prajñā simply pops the balloon and brings us back to where we are. We could say that prajñā is a means to sober up, which is one reason why it is not so popular, because we usually enjoy being intoxicated by our ego trips in saṃsāra. Prajñā cuts through all our attempts at taking credit for being a good Buddhist, being on the path, or having attained something. The prajñāpāramitā sūtras describe all kinds of situations on the path where bodhisattvas can get mired down. At each turn the sūtras say, "You cannot really hang on to that either. No matter how good you think it is, no matter how great you think you are, no matter how fantastic an insight may be, let go and keep moving."

Prajñā also includes the quality of compassion, but it is a somewhat merciless kind of compassion in that it cuts through wherever it is needed. It is not the type of "idiot compassion" that just wants us to feel better, but it cuts through what needs to be exposed or what we need to let go of. In brief, prajñā questions everything that we are, everything that we think, everything that we perceive, and everything that we value. Prajñā is the ultimate destroyer of our value systems, which is another reason why it is not so popular. Thus, prajñā cuts not only through delusion, but also through any tricky attempts by our ego to take credit for being on the path of a bodhisattva or the like. As the prajñāpāramitā sūtras never tire of emphasizing, any colorful fancies of personalized spiritual attainments must be seen through and recognized to be as groundless as everything else. This spotlight quality of prajñā is symbolized by the flames on the sword illuminating our blind spots.

In this way prajñā functions like a stage spotlight, highlighting the main actor. In our personal dramas, the leading actor or actress is of course always "me," and then there are the supporting actors whom we call "others." Prajñā serves to spot and highlight this main actor "me," but the problem here is that the main actor *is* the blind spot in the show. Of course, the main actor does not realize that (and mostly does not want to realize it either), but through prajñā this actor "me" will become a little more self-conscious because the spotlight shines on him or her all the time. There is a sense of no escape. We can no longer hide from ourselves or pretend to be unaware of what is going on in our mind.

Generally ignorance is of two types. The passive type is not knowing something and then googling it, but there is also an active part to ignorance, which means that we do not *want* to see or know, even if we could. In particular, we often do not want to know what is going on in our own mind or what is in its storehouse. As someone recently said, "My mind is like a bad neighborhood, I usually avoid going there alone." That is our ignorance actively avoiding our own mind, avoiding other people, difficult situations, and so on. Prajñā also functions as the direct antidote to these more active tendencies of our ignorance, which does not want us to look too closely at ourselves and what we do. In this sense, prajñā entails both an illuminating quality and a sense of courage to face whatever is going on in our own mind and whatever is happening in any situation. Therefore, we need some courage to really hold the sword of prajñā and wield it skillfully.

Often we think that knowledge or insight means to come up with all the right answers, but prajñā is more like asking all the right questions. Often the question *is* the answer, or much better than any answer. Often one answer just produces ten new questions and trying to get all the right answers down may simply create more reference points in our mind and thus more rigidity and problems. We may think, "Now I understand this really well," but this often just means to expand the territory of our Planet Ego because "I know," "I got it." We simply add one more item to our collection of things that we "know." That is why Zen talks about "Don't-know mind." Of course this does not mean to simply be stupid, but to let go of trying to own anything, let go of "our" knowledge, and let go of "our" achievements. If we really have certain insights and achievements, we will not lose them anyway, but if we hold on to them and become puffed up, they turn into a problem.

To let prajñā unfold in a natural way means to give our basic inquisitiveness more space for its natural acute freshness and to start its own process of inquiry rather than following the beaten track. The teachings on prajñāpāramitā are a clear message not to restrict prajñā to merely rearranging or expanding our web of dualistic categories. Thus, the prajñāpāramitā sūtras say:

> If you think, "I cultivate prajñā," "Prajñā is this," or "It is for the sake of such and such," this may well be prajñā, but it is not prajñāpāramitā.

Since prajñāpāramitā stands for directly encountering ultimate reality, it is the main highway to liberation and omniscience. Therefore, to be immersed in it is explained to be the supreme of all practices and realizations. This is why its qualities as well as its profound and far-reaching impact on our minds cannot be overestimated and are repeatedly praised in the scriptures. They declare that to rest for a single moment within prajñāpāramitā is of far greater merit than—and in fact includes—all other pāramitās, such as generosity. The *Brahmaviśeṣacintiparipṛcchāsūtra* declares:

> Not reflecting is generosity.
> Not abiding in any difference is ethics.
> Not making any distinctions is patience.
> Not adopting or rejecting anything is vigor.
> Not being attached is samādhi.
> Not conceptualizing is prajñā.

Obviously, this is quite different from the usual explanations of what the six pāramitās are. Here they are presented in terms of their connection to prajñāpāramitā or how they manifest as prajñāpāramitā. Generosity is not to reflect, which means to act spontaneously for the benefit of others without premeditation or bias. Ethics means not abiding in any differences in terms of what is proper or improper behavior. If we make any such differences, we are still biased; it is not proper Buddhist ethics or discipline since we still cling to dos and don'ts. From a prajñā point of view, we are still stuck in dualism. True patience means not making any distinctions between what harms and what benefits us or between favorable and unfavorable conditions, but resting in the equality of all phenomena. Vigor, or joyful effort, means not to get stuck in adopting what is considered virtuous and rejecting what is considered nonvirtuous, but engaging in activities for the benefit of others as the natural expression of having realized the emptiness, equality, and primordial purity of all phenomena. Samādhi is meditative equipoise in the sense of mind resting freely in itself without anything to hold on to, without feeling attracted or averse to anything, and without any need to obtain or run away from anything. Prajñā means not to conceptualize "the three spheres" of agent, object, and interaction with regard to anything (such as a giver, a recipient, and the act of giving). Thus, it is completely free from any reference points and discursiveness. If we engage in the pāramitās in that way, we are uniting the two realities—the ultimate and the seeming, or relative, realities.

It is also stated that dwelling in prajñāpāramitā is far superior to any studies, reflections, or other meditations on the dharma, even if these are performed for many eons. It is also the supreme way of making offerings, taking refuge in the three jewels, generating bodhicitta, and purifying all negativities. Both the sūtras and their commentaries describe many signs that indicate increasing familiarity and ease with prajñāpāramitā. In brief, we are able to see much more clearly in any given situation and to deal more carefully and compassionately with both ourselves and with others. We mindfully engage in virtuous actions, afflictions become weaker, the dharma is practiced wholeheartedly, and distractions are relinquished. Clinging in general is reduced, particularly the attachment to this life.

On the positive side of prajñā destroying or undermining everything that we know, and that we need to give up all our concepts, the whole point is to arrive at a state of mind in which we do not cling. Maybe just for a split second we do not really try to achieve anything or to avoid anything. At that point we do not think, "So what now?" We need to look at that very state of mind in which we do not hold on to anything, in which we have no agenda at all, and then see what it is like. Emptiness is not about some *thing* called "emptiness" that we have to realize, but it is about letting go of everything that prevents us from realizing what the true nature of our mind actually is. The nature of the mind is something extremely simple and extremely close. This is the problem because we do not like simple things. We always like sophisticated things, the more sophisticated the better. That is why we create all our preconceived ideas and reference points, our values and belief systems. Sooner or later we are lost and we do not even know our own mind anymore. The teachings on emptiness (and prajñāpāramitā as what realizes emptiness) are trying to make us come back to the natural state of our mind, without all the artificial constructs in it. We do not have to make up the nature of the mind or alter it in any way. The only thing to do is to deconstruct, or let go of our constructs, tearing down our mental sand castles and not clinging to them.

Lady Prajñāpāramitā—Intuition Embracing Intellect

Iconographically prajñāpāramitā is represented as a female deity. She is yellow in color, sits in a cross-legged position, and has four arms, with her upper left hand holding a text, her upper right hand raising a flaming sword, and the lower two arms being in the gesture of meditation. Respectively these represent the three types of prajñā: knowledge through study, cutting through and illuminating delusion, and direct insight into the true nature of all phenomena. These are also called the prajñās resulting from study, reflection, and meditation, which represent a progression from the conceptual and coarse forms of prajñā to its most subtle and nonconceptual form.

Question: When the *Heart Sūtra* says "no ignorance, no termination of ignorance up to no aging and death and no termination of aging and death" and so on, is it meant to help break up our dualistic thinking and to trick us out of it? When I say these words it is helpful to me and it leads me to this unanswerable or mystery place which is somehow quieting. Can you speak to that a bit?

KB: Magical Mystery Tours? Yes, that is definitely one purpose of the *Heart Sūtra*—breaking through our usual concepts. Actually this works on many different levels since there are more coarse concepts and more subtle ones. But even on a very coarse level of concepts, just saying "no eye, no ear, no nose," and so on is already very contrary to what we usually think. We do not think in terms of "no eye, no ear, no nose." We think, "There is an eye, there is a nose, there is an ear." Even on that superficial level the words of the sūtra go against the grain of our habitual tendencies and shake our world. That is the beginning of poking holes into our otherwise so solid and tightly woven cocoon of delusion. Even one tiny hole lets a little bit of fresh air and light into our stale and gloomy cocoon, which is the first step toward freedom. The further we take that, the more profound it gets and we can link it with deeper contemplation and analysis, thus penetrating what "no eye, no ear, no nose" actually means and how it relates to our deeply ingrained habitual tendencies of taking things to be really existent subject and objects. At the same time, we can use the recitation of these words as a direct meditation because we can look at our mind while we say them. How does our mind react when we say "no eye, no ear, no nose"? Does it freak out? Does it show resistance? Does it just get bored? All Buddhist teachings, and the *Heart Sūtra* is no exception, are not intended as mere objects to be studied, but as mirrors that reflect our mind. Therefore, the most important point whenever we study, recite, or reflect on something is to watch how our mind is reacting to it while doing so.

Question: I am wondering why the sūtra is often recited or chanted in a monotone, such as in English and Japanese?

KB: There are different traditions. I cannot really say much about the Zen tradition, but the English version seems to follow the way it is mostly chanted in that tradition. Though it is a monotone, if we do it properly, with the right beat, so to speak, it actually has a lot of power. It can be completely boring or it can be very powerful, like a drumbeat, even without a drum. It depends on us whether it becomes an electrifying wake-up call or just something that puts us to sleep.

Question: My perception is that by avoiding inflection we do not bring any meaning into it other than whatever its essence is.

KB: That is true, you could see the monotone as not only *symbolizing* the emptiness and equality of all phenomena, but as a gate to actually *experience* some sense of equality and "the sound of emptiness," which is the sūtra's essential message. Again, it is important to look at your mind while you recite it in that way and see how your mind resonates (in both a literal and metaphoric sense) with the sound, the beat, the words, and their meaning.

Question: If the buddhas do not speak a word, how do they communicate with sentient beings?

KB: It depends on your view, but from the mahāyāna point of view there are different levels of communication between someone like a buddha and sentient beings. The most superficial level is through speech or physical gestures, but the most fundamental level is between one buddha nature and the other, that is, a buddha's buddha nature communicating with our buddha nature. That is where the actual show is happening. Anything else that seems to be happening on the more conventional level in terms of speech, words, letters, and so on is like a mirror. Obviously, for ordinary sentient beings, it is very difficult (though not entirely impossible) to have a conscious direct communication between a buddha's buddha nature and their own buddha nature, so there needs to be some kind of "mirror" for that. In this way, all the teachings as we know them are like mirrors for our own buddha nature. Whatever text we see, whatever teachings we hear, whatever teachers we might meet, they are like mirrors. So we should not get stuck in just looking at them, but rather look at our own mind in its interaction with the teachings and the teachers.

The manner in which ordinary beings interact with buddhas or buddha nature for most of the path is that the mind of the student takes on the form of the teaching. From that point of view something like this piece of paper with its letters is not really something outside or material, but it is our own mind appearing in the form of what we call "paper." When we look at this paper with some Buddhist teaching on it, it is trying to tell us to look back at our own mind. The same goes for meditation. For example, if we visualize a deity, that is also a mirror for the nature of our mind. Finally, when we do not need a mirror anymore, but see our mind or our buddha nature as it is, we are a buddha.

Generally, when we look into a mirror, we are not interested so much in the mirror itself, but we are interested in what we want to see in the mirror, usually our face. Likewise, when we look at the teachings or a teacher, the main thing is what we see in ourselves and not so much what we see "outside." That is the whole point of the Buddhist teaching, it always is to be applied to our mind. That is why it is not really a philosophy or some theory. No matter what the teaching is, it is something to be mixed with and worked out in our own mind. After all, this was the project of the Buddha—to show other people the nature of their mind through their own experience and engagement.

Question: This is a question about walking the line between the relative and the absolute. Sometimes I find that I do not have bodhicitta, I lack devotion, or I simply behave badly according to the guidelines of Buddhism. Then I feel very frustrated, but sometimes I find that when I reflect on the emptiness teachings, I can suddenly relax. However, I am not sure if that is the right approach. Let's say I have no bodhicitta, and I try so hard, but nothing comes from it. And then I say, "Okay, forget it, it is just emptiness, why try so hard?" Then I feel relaxed, but there is also some uncertainty about whether this approach will actually help me or harm me more.

KB: Fundamentally, it is never wrong to relax, especially on the Buddhist path. The Mahāmudrā tradition says that those who relax the most will have the best meditation, those who relax to a middling degree, will have middling meditation, and you can imagine what happens to the rest. Relaxation is really what emptiness is for, believe it or not. The experience of emptiness is the most relaxed state of mind we can possibly have. Therefore, if we tap into that or connect with it, that is not wrong at all because that is what the nature of our mind is—fundamental openness, ease, and spaciousness. In that nature of the mind there is nothing that we have to do or should not do. Obviously this is very different from misunderstanding emptiness as just being some state of indifference, in which we do not care about anything. Also, until we are able to realize that ultimate state, all the relative Buddhist practices are aids that are geared toward helping us relax in this most fundamental way.

Thus, practically speaking, to bring the ultimate view, or the emptiness aspect, into relative practices does not necessarily or primarily mean to logically analyze them as to their lack of intrinsic nature, but to relax about what we are doing and not to be so uptight, workaholic, and instant-success-minded. We also need to see whether these practices actually help us to relax or whether our mind just gets more paranoid and tense. If it does or if we become totally frustrated, this is a clear indication that it is time to relax. As long as we are on the path it is of course very difficult to unify the two levels of reality (ultimate and relative, or seeming) all the time. That is why we typically bounce back and forth between the two, sometimes emphasizing the relative and sometimes the ultimate. On the path that is fine because by doing so they enhance each other. If we are tired or frustrated, we relax and let go of trying so hard. Once we have relaxed, we can give our relative practices another shot and ideally carry over a little bit of our relaxation into our next attempt at whatever practice we do. This is how to bring together the view and the conduct or the two truths. If we do all those practices in Buddhism without being relaxed at least to some extent, they do not work very well. The Buddhist path is not some kind of twelve-step program. It is meant to help our mind to be at ease. Also, we do not have to practice every single one of the many methods in Buddhism. Sometimes, if a practice really does not work for us and our mind just gets more and more uptight, maybe we need another method.

Prajñāpāramitā as Ground, Path, and Fruition

Now, to continue with a more detailed presentation of prajñāpāramitā, the texts usually distinguish four types, or aspects, of prajñāpāramitā. That is, if we say "prajñāpāramitā," it means one of four things— (1) natural prajñāpāramitā, (2) scriptural prajñāpāramitā, (3) the prajñāpāramitā of the path, or (4) fruitional prajñāpāramitā. Dignāga's *Prajñāpāramitārthasaṃgraha* describes this as follows:

> Prajñāpāramitā is nondual wisdom,
> Which is the Tathāgata.
> By virtue of being connected to this actuality to be accomplished,
> It is also the term for both the scriptures and the path.[4]

Natural prajñāpāramitā is nondual wisdom, which is the same as the fruition—a buddha or tathāgata. By virtue of being connected to mind's natural wisdom and its full manifestation (what is to be accomplished), the scriptures that are related to prajñāpāramitā and the path that leads to the fruition are also labeled as "prajñāpāramitā." According to the Eighth Karmapa's commentary on the prajñāpāramitā sūtras, (1) *natural* or *actual prajñāpāramitā* is defined as "suchness, which is never something other and bears the name 'wisdom that lacks the duality of apprehender and apprehended.'" So there are two aspects of natural prajñāpāramitā. On the one hand, it is the true nature of all phenomena, but it is not just an object. It is also that which perceives this nature— the nonconceptual nondual wisdom in which there is no separation between subject and object or perceiver and perceived. When this suchness is obscured by various conditioned elements, it is given the name "the basic element that is the sugata heart." In other words, the Karmapa says that buddha nature and natural prajñāpāramitā are just different names for the same thing.

Once this natural wisdom or buddha nature has become free from all its fetters or obscurations, it is called (4) *fruitional prajñāpāramitā*— the wisdom of a tathāgata, which is inseparable from the dharmakāya or

---

4   D3809, verse 1.

buddhahood. So this nondual wisdom already exists in all sentient beings as the natural prajñāpāramitā and is merely uncovered on the path.

(2) The *scriptural prajñāpāramitā*, which teaches this meaning, is "the mind that appears as assemblies of names, words, and letters, and is suitable to be observed in the disciples' consciousnesses that entail dualistic appearances." This definition of scriptural prajñāpāramitā is similar to the above definition of the dharma of scriptures. Again, the scriptures are not said to be matter, such as ink and paper, but what appears as such under the influence of a buddha or bodhisattva in the minds of those students who still have dualistic appearances. For this is the only way they can perceive the teachings, in this case, the prajñāpāramitā sūtras and their commentaries.

(3) The *prajñāpāramitā of the path* is "the prajñāpāramitā that arises as the nature of nonconceptual wisdom when resting in meditative equipoise." Strictly speaking, this only happens from the first bodhisattva bhūmi onward. However, in a wider sense it refers to any insight, even a glimpse, into the true nature of phenomena from the very start of the path. Of course in the beginning that wisdom or insight is not nonconceptual, it is still conceptual. Nevertheless, it is referred to as prajñā, though it is not yet the pāramitā of prajñā. It is like baby prajñā, which has to grow up.

Sometimes the texts also speak about a mere reflection of prajñāpāramitā, which refers to the wisdoms of śrāvakas and pratyekabuddhas. The prajñāpāramitā sūtras say that śrāvakas and pratyekabuddhas too rely in their practice on nothing but prajñāpāramitā, but they are not aware that it is prajñāpāramitā, nor do they call it that. Generally, the mahāyāna says that any realization which we can have on the path comes from working with prajñāpāramitā.

The Prajñāpāramitā Sūtras

From among those four types of prajñāpāramitā, let's discuss the scriptural prajñāpāramitā, that is, the sūtras, in more detail. According to the mahāyāna, the prajñāpāramitā sūtras were taught by Buddha Śākyamuni on this mountain near Rājagrha, but it is said that they were not valued enough afterwards, so they disappeared for about four hundred years and were not circulated anymore. Later, Nāgārjuna retrieved them from the nāgas. Nāgas are a whole class of beings who, technically speaking, fall under the category of animals in Buddhism. In the West we find them in mythology or fairy tales described as dragons, toads underneath the earth, or serpentlike creatures such as Hydra with her many heads. Usually nāgas like all valuable things and collect and store them. The particular nāgas who were the caretakers of the prajñāpāramitā sūtras are said to live in the ocean and somehow Nāgārjuna talked them into giving them to him.

There are many different prajñāpāramitā sūtras, very long ones and very short ones. The Tibetan canon contains twenty-three such sūtras, ranging from one hundred thousand lines down to a single syllable (the Chinese canon has even more prajñāpāramitā sūtras). If we look at the sheer volume of these prajñāpāramitā sūtras, they make up twenty percent (twenty-one volumes) of the entire Tibetan canon of all Buddhist sūtras and tantras together. In the Tibetan tradition, the main prajñāpāramitā sūtras among these twenty-three are called "the six mothers and the eleven children." The six "mother" prajñāpāramitā sūtras are easy to remember because we just have to remember the numbers of their lines—one hundred thousand, twenty-five thousand, eighteen thousand, ten thousand, and eight thousand lines, and the *Prajñāpāramitāsaṃcayagāthā* (a condensed versified version of the latter sūtra). The *Heart Sūtra* is one among "the eleven children."

All of these sūtras say pretty much the same thing, it is just a matter of how much detail they go into. In the *Heart Sūtra* we have all those lists of things, like "no eye," "no ear," and so on. In the large sūtras those lists are extended dramatically, so we have hundreds of pages where it says "no this, no that." That is why, sometimes, they are a little bit tedious to read and it is easy to fall asleep. However, the point of reading these sūtras was never to serve as some kind of light bedtime reading. They are intended as contemplation manuals with greater or lesser detail, which are to be read again and again. But the sūtras do not only give all those lists, they also talk about the path of the bodhisattva in terms of what to cultivate. At the same time, they keep telling us at every corner not to cling to anything that we cultivate, realize, or attain. For example, some sūtras give extensive explanations on generating bodhicitta, but say at the same time that bodhisattvas do not make their home in bodhicitta or the generation of bodhicitta. In this way, the prajñāpāramitā sūtras are not only talking about ultimate reality, but also about relative reality and relative practice, though always in connection with the ultimate view. Typically, all these sūtras are presented in the form of dialogues, except for the one in a single letter, which is really a monologue. Also, often it is not the Buddha himself who is teaching, but somebody else, such as Avalokiteśvara doing the job in the *Heart Sūtra*. The Buddha just says "good job" at the end. In other sūtras there are several people who teach. One of the main teachers is a śrāvaka named Subhūti, who has many dialogues with Śāriputra. In the early Buddhist tradition Śāriputra is the wisest of all the students of the Buddha, but in the prajñāpāramitā sūtras he is given a hard time. He is always the one who asks questions or raises qualms, either not really understanding things or at least pretending not to. Then Subhūti or someone else answers, sometimes with a counterquestion, and then the dialogue goes back and forth.

In this way, most sūtras in general are records or transcripts of teachings or dialogues, just as we have our transcripts today. The sūtras are either teachings by the Buddha himself or by people who were authorized or blessed by the Buddha. For example, at the beginning of the *Heart Sūtra* the Buddha goes into samādhi. Then both Śāriputra's question and Avalokiteśvara's answer occur by virtue of being blessed by the Buddha's mind in deep meditation.

When the prajñāpāramitā sūtras came to Tibet, they were mainly translated during the early translation period in the eighth and ninth centuries CE and then revised several times. Distinct traditions of interpreting the prajñāpāramitā sūtras also developed. There are not only the Indian commentaries on the sūtras themselves, but a lot of commentaries on a text by Maitreya called *The Ornament of Clear Realization* (*Abhisamayālaṃkāra*). This text is basically like a zip file of the prajñāpāramitā sūtras, being an extreme condensation of the sūtra in twenty-five thousand lines. It is more like a table of contents or a brief memo, often just saying, "A, B, C, . . ." There is little chance of understanding this text without comparing it to the sūtra in twenty-five thousand lines in order to see what it is talking about. Eventually this text and its Indian and Tibetan commentaries became the primary bases for the interpretation of the prajñāpāramitā sūtras in Tibet.

Complicated Simplicity

As for the principal topics of the prajñāpāramitā sūtras, there are two. The obvious one is, of course, emptiness—back and forth, up and down, left and right, and all over the place. This is the explicit teaching of these sūtras, their obvious subject matter. But there is also their hidden meaning, which consists of the progression of the paths and bhūmis of bodhisattvas. In other words, the emptiness teaching speaks about the object or what is to be realized, while the teachings on paths and bhūmis speak about the subject that perceives that object, that is, what happens in the minds of bodhisattvas when they actually meditate on and realize emptiness, from the level of a beginner all the way up to buddhahood. In this way, the prajñāpāramitā sūtras explain both sides of the coin. They are not just saying that everything is empty and after that it is "Good luck!" They also give instructions on how to work with this emptiness, how to contemplate it, and how to realize it.

In the commentarial tradition, the emptiness teachings of the prajñāpāramitā sūtras are mainly discussed and thoroughly established through reasoning in the Madhyamaka literature, while *The Ornament of Clear Realization* and its commentaries are regarded as the commentaries on the sūtras' hidden topic of path and bhūmis. The commentarial literature on *The Ornament of Clear Realization* consists of twenty-one Indian texts and many hundreds in Tibet. This is an interesting process because first we have these very long prajñāpāramitā sūtras, which hardly anybody can study and understand properly even in an entire lifetime. Then Maitreya composed this "in-a-nutshell" text of *The Ornament of Clear Realization* in 273 verses, but we cannot understand that either because it is too short. So Indian and Tibetan masters wrote commentaries on this short text, which means that they unzipped the zip file again. But that in turn resulted in a mass of commentarial literature even larger than the original sūtras.

In a way this is ironic when we think about what these sūtras talk about, which is emptiness. Emptiness is the simplest and most unelaborated thing we could imagine, but then there is this whole literature about all these very discursive details with all their subpoints. There are five paths and ten bhūmis, and each path is divided into a number of stages, with certain numbers of obscurations having to be relinquished on each one of those subpaths. Most people just think, "Who wants or needs to know all that? Don't we have too many thoughts already? I thought this was about letting go of all reference points." Of course nobody really wants to know all those details and in a sense we all know them already, because they are the details of the many reference points that we already have in our mind. The fact that these sūtras and their commentaries talk about our obscurations is precisely the point why they seem so endless and complicated—because our minds are complicated. Emptiness is extremely simple, but our convoluted minds that do not get this simplicity are very complicated. It is not that the Buddha and the other speakers in the sūtras and the commentaries really like to, but they need to address each one of those knots in our minds, which are like knots in space. There are a lot of knots in the space of our minds, so when we address all of them, we end up with all those big books. When we read those books, we may find that we do not really have a particular knot in our mind, but I am sure we will find plenty of the others that are described. Also, we often may not be aware of being on a particular trip and pretend to ourselves that we do not have certain hang-ups, even if it is obvious to everyone else that we do. This conundrum is nicely expressed by the Western philosopher Wittgenstein, who said:

> Why is philosophy so complicated? It ought to be *entirely* simple. Philosophy unties the knots in our thinking that we have, in a senseless way, put there. To do this it must make movements as complicated as these knots are. Although the *results* of philosophy are simple, its method cannot be, if it is to succeed. The complexity of philosophy is not its subject matter, but our knotted understanding.[5]

5   Cited in K. T. Fann, *Wittgenstein's Conception of Philosophy* (Berkeley: University of California Press, 1969), p. 103, n. 4.

This is interesting because it is exactly what the Buddha said and what is taught in the prajñāpāramitā texts. If we read the sūtras, they are not simple at all. If we read Madhyamaka texts, they are even more difficult. And if we read *The Ornament of Clear Realization* and its commentaries, they are even worse than Madhyamaka texts. Nevertheless, it is important to see the reason why all these texts are so complicated. It is not because the subject matter is complicated, but because our minds are so complicated. If we want to unravel all the knots in our minds, there are different approaches. We can try to unravel them one by one and then it takes a lot of time and we get into all the nitty-gritty details. Of course there are other approaches where we just try to cut through the Gordian knot of our mind with one blow. As far as the prajñāpāramitā sūtras go, the approach is gradual and not sudden. They also talk about a sudden approach, but only for certain very advanced people. For most people, to unravel their knots is a gradual path, which consists of what we call the five paths, the ten bhūmis, and so on.

When the Tibetan tradition speaks about "prajñāpāramitā" as a topic, it means *The Ornament of Clear Realization* and its commentaries, that is, the topic of paths and bhūmis. Madhyamaka is a separate topic and solely concerned about emptiness, though, as explained above, the two topics are complementary. However, Mādhyamikas hardly ever talk about paths and bhūmis, they are simply not interested in the details of the conventions of the path on the level of relative reality. They just talk about emptiness, back and forth, and then it is "Good luck!" after that. They usually do not even talk about how to meditate on emptiness. There are a few texts by Mādhyamikas that discuss meditation, but usually they do not go there.

Just to note, the *Chö* teachings of the Tibetan yoginī Machig Labdrön are said to be prajñāpāramitā in essence, but to also accord with vajrayāna principles, thus combining both sūtra and tantra. According to Jamgön Kongtrul, the way in which the *Chö* teachings are related to prajñāpāramitā is that prajñāpāramitā is like the earth, or the ground, on which we cut down a tree. If we have no ground, there is neither any tree to cut down nor do we have a working basis. Likewise, prajñāpāramitā is the ground for cutting through ego-inflating thoughts that bind us in saṃsāra. This cutting-through has to have some ground where it happens, which is prajñāpāramitā.

Prajñāpāramitā as a Buddhist Heresy

One of the difficult features of the prajñāpāramitā sūtras is that they contrast with the earlier more foundational Buddhist teachings. The prajñāpāramitā sūtras seem to dump all the hallmarks and holy cows of foundational Buddhism, such as the five skandhas, the twelve links of dependent origination, the four noble truths, nirvāṇa, and so on. They all go down the drain, so to speak. In early Buddhism, at some point, there developed a tendency toward an overly scholastic and reifying approach to the teachings. Scholars put everything that the Buddha said in categories with many subcategories and all kinds of conceptual interrelations. They constructed this huge closet with a lot of drawers and subdrawers, and everything had to fit somewhere. Their understanding was that reality is made up of many different things, all of which exist truly and ultimately. This ultrarealistic approach with its lists of "dharmas," or phenomena, is called *abhidharma*. It is this abhidharma tradition with all of its classifications and subclassifications and a strong tendency to solidify everything that is one of the main targets of the deconstructive approach of the prajñāpāramitā sūtras. Thus, the prajñāpāramitā sūtras are counteracting the tendency to overly reify the Buddha's teachings through putting everything into neat categories and thinking that this is how the world actually exists.

Edward Conze, one of the few pioneers of translating the prajñāpāramitā sūtras and studying them, said that there are five main points in which the mahāyāna approach of the prajñāpāramitā sūtras and early Buddhism differ. First, the ideals, the aims, and the career of a bodhisattva are different from the arhat. Arhats are primarily interested in self-liberation, whereas bodhisattvas strive for liberating all sentient beings, in fact making them become buddhas and not just arhats. That involves the motivation of bodhicitta, the wish to attain completely perfect buddhahood for the sake of benefiting all beings. The main point in that motivation of bodhicitta is the wish to liberate other sentient beings from their suffering—bodhisattvas do not wish to attain buddhahood for their own sake. That is very important because usually we think that the main point in bodhicitta is to become a buddha, but that is still very ego-oriented. The actual core of the bodhisattva vow or bodhicitta is the wish to be able to free all beings from suffering and it is only for that goal that bodhisattvas strive to attain buddhahood, because buddhahood is the most powerful and efficient state to help beings become free from suffering. In other words, from the perspective of bodhicitta, buddhahood is just a means to an end, but not an end in itself. In fact, it is not an end at all because buddhahood is when our job of helping sentient beings *really* starts full scale.

Second, the wisdom in the prajñāpāramitā sūtras is contrasted with the wisdom in the foundational teachings, which is the wisdom of realizing that there is no personal self or of realizing the four noble truths. This wisdom is only directed toward one's own five skandhas and sees that there is no self in these skandhas, whereas the wisdom in the prajñāpāramitā sūtras is much more extensive. This wisdom looks at the skandhas of all sentient beings as well as all other phenomena, inside and outside, seeing that none of all these phenomena has a nature of its own.

Third, the prajñāpāramitā sūtras say that bodhisattvas should not review phenomena, which means not getting stuck on any character-istics of phenomena or solidifying them, whereas in the abhidharma everything is classified according to its characteristics into long lists, which are cross-referenced and become more and more reified.

Fourth, in the abhidharma the principle of impermanence, one of the hallmarks of the foundational approach of Buddhism, is consid-ered a key point to be realized. A main approach was to investigate the momentariness of things, that is, the arising, abiding, and ceasing of phenomena, and to describe that process. In contrast, the prajñāpāramitā sūtras constantly say that there is no arising, no abiding, and no ceasing. Thus, one of the hallmarks of these sūtras is that "all phenomena are unborn," which means they never really come into existence in the first place and thus are empty of any true arising, any inherent existence, and any ceasing.

Fifth, the abhidharma speaks about a multiplicity of phenomena as making up reality; even ultimate reality consists of multiple phenomena, such as minute material particles and smallest moments of mind, all of which are truly existent. The prajñāpāramitā sūtras say that there are no multiple phenomena because there are no phenomena in the first place. Also, there are no separate phenomena since we cannot establish any hard and fast distinctions or boundaries between them. All such distinctions are nothing but completely arbitrary conceptual labels. For example, we think that the cushion and the mat it lies on are two different and separate things, but for a small child this is not obvious at all. We also think that this table and the carpet are different, but in terms of our visual perception, that is not obvious either. If we just take what appears in our visual field, who says that whatever appears left, right, above, and below in it is really different? We could just as well take our entire visual field as one multicolored object, which is what our visual consciousness shows us. It is only through our imputations and labels that we distinguish between different objects. Our eyes just see everything in this room as a big multicolored patch, but then our conceptual mind draws boundaries, such as there being different people sitting on different cushions and chairs, wearing different clothes, and so on.

Groundless Paths

During what is experienced on the mental path of refining and uncovering prajñāpāramitā, prajñā in itself is completely beyond all reification, inconceivable, and inexpressible, yet its realization is to be progressively cultivated. Traditionally such experiences and realizations are discussed in the technical framework of "paths and bhūmis," which framework represents the hidden meaning of the prajñāpāramitā sūtras. In Buddhism, "paths" and "bhūmis" primarily refer to the inner spiritual development of the mind, that is, our mind traveling in its own space and arriving at its own nature ("mind" is sometimes even given as a synonym for "path"). In other words, this refers to the continuum of cultivating and familiarizing with certain states of mind and insights in many different ways, from the beginner level up through perfect buddhahood, which entails increasingly positive and powerful mental qualities.

The Sanskrit word *mārga* for "path" derives from the verbal root *mārg* ("to seek for," "to strive after," "to trace out," "to go" or "to move") and has a wide range of meanings, such as "(right) way," "path," "course," "channel"; "search," "inquiry"; "method," "style," "practice"; and "hinting at" or "indicating how something is to happen." In other words, the whole path is about searching: we are searching for questions, we are searching for answers, and we are searching for what is the true nature of reality. Since *mārga* can also mean "hinting at or indicating how something is happening," the path includes both the traveler and the travel guide—it consists not only of our search, but also of the hints that we receive for our search from a teacher, which are like pointing fingers.

The five Buddhist paths can be described through the analogy of a journey to a nice scenic picnic place. First, we need to get our equipment together, such as our picnic basket, different kinds of food, gas for the car, and so on. That corresponds to the path of accumulation (or equipment) on which we gather the gear for our travel. Next, we get into our car and drive on the road toward our picnic spot. Of course, we have already read our guidebook, so while we are getting closer, we are well oriented and keep imagining the place that is our destination. If we read our guidebook very well, we can bring this place to mind quite clearly, though we are not there yet. That is the path of preparation. In a sense, we are working here with the fruition, but in a conceptual manner. Nevertheless, through this, we are getting closer to our final destination. Eventually, we arrive at that place and we can look at the wonderful scenery, which is like the path of seeing—we directly see the place in front of us for the first time and we need no more guidebooks. While we hang out at this place and walk around, we explore and become more and more familiar with the details of the landscape and its surroundings. We are not moving on to yet another place, but we become acquainted with every tree, every rock, every flower, and so on of our picnic spot. That is the path of meditation, or familiarization, on which we become thoroughly familiar with all the details and facets of what we already saw in a more general way when we arrived at this place for the first time. Finally, we know the place inside out. We feel completely at home and are able to get around in it as we please. We remember every aspect of it and can even describe it to others in perfect detail. This is the path of no more learning, or the final result of the path.

On the path to buddhahood how do we practice with the prajñāpāramitā sūtras? Apart from the more technical aspects of the five paths and the ten bhūmis, in terms of actually experiencing prajñāpāramitā, the whole point of the progressive and profound realizations on these paths and bhūmis is to become friends with the basic groundlessness of our existence and the notion of no-path. This principle applies not only to saṃsāric, or afflicted, phenomena, but also to nirvāṇic, or purified, phenomena, such as any and all experiences, realizations, and conduct on the entire path up through the ultimate fruition of omniscient buddhahood. Both the explicit and the implicit subject matter of the prajñāpāramitā sūtras—emptiness and the path of realizing it—are aptly summarized by Edward Conze:

> The thousands of lines of the Prajñāpāramitā can be summed up in the following two sentences: 1) One should become a Bodhisattva (or, Buddha-to-be), i.e. one who is content with nothing less than all-knowledge attained through the perfection of wisdom for the sake of all beings. 2) There is no such thing as a Bodhisattva, or as all-knowledge, or as a 'being', or as the perfection of wisdom, or as an attainment. To accept both these contradictory facts is to be perfect.[6]

Or as Gareth Sparham puts it:

> According to Hari[bhadra], the message of the *Perfection of Wisdom Sūtras* is that the entire path and its result operate on a covering level made up of illusory mind, while below, as it were, at an ultimate level, they are empty of any essential nature.[7]

Nāgārjuna's *Bodhisambhāra* simply says:

6   Edward Conze, *The Prajñāpāramitā Literature* ('s Gravenhage: Mouton and Co., 1960), p. 15.
7   Gareth Sparham, trans., *Abhisamayālaṃkāra with Vṛtti and Ālokā*, vol. 1: First Abhisamaya (Fremont, Calif.: Jain Publishing Company, 2006), p. xxvii.

Bodhisattvas benefit sentient beings,
But do not see any sentient beings.
This is indeed a very difficult point,
Superb and ungraspable.[8]

In terms of the actual practice on the path of a bodhisattva, however, it is not simply a matter of "accepting contradictory facts." Rather, this path means to gain an increasingly thorough understanding of each one of the two realities—seeming and ultimate—and eventually realize that they are not two separate levels of existence, but the different outlooks of the confused dualistic minds of ordinary beings versus the nonreferential wisdom minds of those who directly experience how things really are, with the former eventually dissolving within the latter as we progress on the path. From this perspective, what may seem to be contradictory is seen not to be so at all. This is called realizing the union of the two realities, or the union of prajñā and skillful means (*upāya*).

Since the prajñāpāramitā sūtras are practice or meditation manuals, it is important to bring together the two levels of reality in our practice. This means to blend what these sūtras teach explicitly—emptiness, or the view of how things actually are—with what we actually do on the path, as extreme and opposite these two may seem at first. But that is the whole idea. The message of the prajñāpāramitā sūtras is not just that everything is empty and that's that, meaning that we do not have to do anything. Rather, bodhisattvas do a lot of things. Therefore, we work on both levels of reality at the same time, though in varying degrees at different stages of the path. As a beginner, we usually go back and forth between trying to remember the view and focusing on what to do practically. But as we progress, those two objects of focus become closer until they become inseparable. This is known as "the union of wisdom and skillful means," which is the hallmark of the mahāyāna path and often compared to the two wings of a bird. It is very hard to fly with one wing, so we need those two wings of wisdom and means. In other words, it is not enough to simply posssess wisdom but we need to apply that wisdom in our life in skillful ways. We do not only consist of mind, but also of body and speech, and we also have

8 Verse 72.

obscurations of body, speech, and mind. Therefore, we need to work with that wisdom or that insight in many different ways in our ordinary day-to-day life in order to benefit both ourselves and others.

Dirt, Soap, and Water

As the Buddha realized, sentient beings are fundamentally confused, which means they do not realize what they really are. It is due to that confusion, which arises from holding on to seemingly solidly and really existing things and persons, that they do all kinds of things that compound their confusion and suffering. Ultimately, to gain true freedom, the main point is to realize that none of this confusion and the ensuing actions and problems really happen. But at the same time, unless we have realized that fully, we need to work with that very confusion in order to skillfully unravel it. This is similar to dreaming and waking up. If we wake up from a nightmare, it is not really a problem anymore, but as long as we are *in* that nightmare, it is good to have some means to work with the nightmare directly, such as training in lucid dreaming and being able to change the dream. That means, first, we need to recognize that it is a dream, but recognition alone does not mean we are out of it already, the dream experience is still there. Next, when we become more skillful, we can actually work with and change the dream, such as talking to, petting, and playing with the tiger that chases us in our nightmare. We are still not awake, but it is much better than just being carried away helplessly by the nightmare experience, such as being eaten by that tiger. In addition, if we work with the dream in that way, it also brings us closer to actually waking up.

Likewise, bodhisattvas recognize that their saṃsāric life is just a dream or an illusion, but at first, though they do not take it for real anymore, this dream still keeps appearing. Therefore, they work with this dream reality, which is much easier now since it is completely fluid and malleable. Finally, they awaken from the nightmare of conditioned existence into the bright sunny daylight of buddhahood. That is why it is important to bring the two levels of reality together in order not to get completely stuck in the dream experience of saṃsāra and work solely on the level of that experience. We always need to keep the larger perspective in mind that what we really want to do is wake up from that dream.

According to the prajñāpāramitā sūtras, in actual fact all afflictions and obscurations as well as their remedies are alike in being completely unreal and without any nature of their own—they never even came into being in the first place. Nevertheless, until this is fully realized and made a living experience, the path consists of applying progressively refined antidotes to progressively subtle obscurations in an illusionlike manner. Eventually we have to let go of even the most refined antidote once its job of seemingly having eliminated its corresponding factor to be relinquished has been accomplished. From the perspective of the true and unchanging nature of phenomena, anything that appears as either something to be relinquished or a remedy is nothing but an adventitious illusory obscuration. However, from the perspective of the path, we need to work on recognizing precisely this fact. As the famous female Chinese Buddhist ancestor Kongshi Daoren wrote in a poem on the wall of a bathhouse:

> If nothing truly exists, what are you bathing? Where could even the slightest bit of dust come from? . . . Even if you see no difference between the water and the dirt, it all must be washed away completely when you enter here.

That basically summarizes the path. Of course, ultimately, there is nothing to do, but when we go under the shower, there are things to do. If we do not feel dirty in the first place, we are fine and there is nothing to do. If there are no concepts of dirt or something that has to be removed and a remedy, there is nothing to do, but once we enter the shower because we feel dirty, we have to do something—we cannot just stay there and remain dirty. Also, even in ordinary terms, when we take a shower we have to relinquish the remedy. When we shower, we use water and soap, which are the remedies for dirt. As Khenpo Tsultrim Gyamtso Rinpoche says, "First, our body is dirty and then we smear some other dirt onto it, which we call 'soap.'" We do not want to leave the dirt on our body, nor do we want to leave the soap (the remedy for the dirt) there either. We are not going into the shower, putting soap on our body, and then stepping out of the shower and putting our clothes on again without having washed the soap off with water. Finally, we want to get rid of the water too (which is a more subtle remedy than soap): we are not getting dressed while we are wet. When we clean our body in this way, we are not really taking anything away from the body itself to make it cleaner, but we are taking away the things that are not our body. We are not taking a shower with hydrochloric acid in order to get *really* clean. It works, but only once.

Likewise, when we wash our laundry, strictly speaking, we are not really washing or cleaning our laundry, but we clean the dirt, because what we still want to keep is our clothes. If washing meant that our laundry, such as a shirt, loses some of its substance, we would be done very soon and would not have any clothes to wear anymore. Again, we wash the dirt through putting some detergent onto it, which is the remedy, and then we rinse it in order to get rid of the remedy. That means, even on an ordinary level, nobody wants to keep the remedies.

Likewise, the remedies on the Buddhist path only serve a purpose as long as they work on their corresponding obscurations to be relinquished. Once they have done that, we need to drop them too. Otherwise, the remedies simply become another problem or obscuration, just as when we continue to take antibiotics when our pneumonia has been cured and we get sick from the antibiotics (if not earlier). From the fundamental point of view of emptiness, both obscurations and their remedies are a problem and neither is really intrinsically better than the other. The only good thing about the remedies is that they resemble the ability to change a lucid dream so that we come closer to eventually waking up. But if we get stuck in just playing around with that lucid dream and become completely absorbed in all the cool things that we can do in it, we will never wake up. It is a better and more entertaining dream, but it is still a dream.

A traditional image of how we work with the obscurations to be relinquished and their remedies is one illusory elephant defeating another illusory elephant. Or it is like a movie where the good guys beat up the bad guys, but actually neither the characters nor the fight were real. Still, it works in the movie and when we get caught up in the story, it works in our mind too, producing all kinds of thoughts, emotions, and even physical reactions. But then, who wants to be in a movie for twenty-four hours a day?

In this vein, Khenpo Tsultrim Gyamtso Rinpoche often says that the Buddhist path is basically nothing but a sequence of more subtle concepts counteracting coarser ones. We start with very thick ideas about ourselves, the world, and everybody else, and then we chop them up or counteract them through more subtle concepts. For example, if we think that things really exist and are lasting, the Buddha taught the remedy of impermanence. But that is not the end, because the prajñāpāramitā sūtras say that impermanence is not ultimate reality either. If we look into impermanence in a deeper way, we end up with emptiness. However, emptiness is not ultimate reality either if we make it into some "thing," such as thinking, "That's it." This is the reason why the Buddha talked about "the emptiness of emptiness." The point here is that whatever level of insight into reality we may have, whether it is an understanding of impermanence or an understanding of emptiness, as long as we hold on to or solidify it, it will not do us much good because it just turns into yet another reference point, yet another hang-up. So "the emptiness of emptiness" just means to let go of any reference points about emptiness itself or the realization of emptiness. If we think we found something, it is certainly not emptiness, so it must be something else. This is why Nāgārjuna's *Mūlamadhyamakakārikā* says:

> The victors taught that emptiness
> Means to eradicate all views,
> But those stuck in emptiness being a view
> Are said to be truly incurable.[9]

The Undoing of Doing

Of course, the prajñāpāramitā sūtras talk all the time about having no reference points and being nondiscursive, but at the same time they are extremely discursive in *talking about* being nondiscursive. However, this discursiveness is due to the people in the audience whose minds

---

9   XIII.8.

are so discursive. Emptiness is the simplest thing ever, as we can see from the prajñāpāramitā sūtra in one letter, which just says "A." There is no discursiveness in that, but then what? What are we going to do with that? Therefore, for most people, a little bit (or a lot) more elaboration is needed. We can choose from among the wide range of longer and shorter prajñāpāramitā sūtras how much elaboration we personally want. Fortunately, we are only talking about the *Heart Sūtra* here and not about the longer ones.

When we consider the language of the prajñāpāramitā sūtras, in modern terms we would call it "deconstructive." Most of what the sūtras teach, at least in terms of emptiness, is not really something that tells us what to do, but it tells us, "Don't do this" and "Don't do that." For example, if we tell somebody, "Put your right foot on your left thigh and your left foot on your right thigh, then put your right hand into your left hand in your lap, and keep your back straight," we are telling them what to do when assuming the physical meditation posture. These instructions involve a lot of conceptualization on our part and we also have to know what all those things such as our feet, our thighs, and our spine are. Such instructions on how to do something are not deconstructive, but if someone says to us, "Don't think" or "Forget it" or "emptiness" or "A," we are not really instructed to *do* anything. We are basically told, "Just stop doing whatever you are doing," but we are not told what to do instead. There is a sense of open-endedness here, which is the typical style of the prajñāpāramitā sūtras that was also adopted in the Ch'an and Zen traditions. They basically perfected it—whatever we think, say or do, they always give us the opposite or something that makes no sense whatsoever.

It is important to keep that in mind when working with the *Heart Sūtra* because usually we are fixated on wanting to hear what we will be doing or what we are supposed to do. If we do not receive instructions on what to do, we get antsy and we wonder, "What is all of this about anyway? I just want to hear what I am supposed to meditate on. I just want to hear what I should do." However, the prajñāpāramitā teachings are very elusive in that regard. They say a lot of things, but most of their statements just serve as means to undermine and cut off our ideas about what to do or what to hang on to. When the *Heart Sūtra* says that there is no eye, no ear, no nose, no mind, no wisdom, no attainment, no nonattainment, and so on, we can feel how our mind keeps jumping back and forth. When we hear "no attainment," we think, "Okay, I get it, there is nothing to be attained." But then the text says "no nonattainment" and we think, "Wait a minute! You just said the opposite. Which one is it?"

So where does that leave us? Where is our mind in between those two mutually exclusive options? If we hear "no attainment and no nonattainment," we are basically left clueless. We are left in a spot where there is nothing to hold on to, which is the whole idea here. Again, this is not so much about realizing that there is *really* no attainment or that there is *really* no nonattainment, but the main point is to look at our mind and how it reacts when all its toys are taken away one by one. What is a toyless mind? What is a mind that does not seek to entertain itself? What is a mind that does not grasp at anything, including itself? This is the fundamental "point of no return" to which the prajñāpāramitā sūtras, the Zen tradition, and other such approaches try to get us. In a sense, they push us to the edge of the cliff of our dualistic conceptual mind and then it is up to us to jump into the groundlessness of "no-mind."

This is why in the Zen tradition we have all those statements such as, "If you see the Buddha on the road, kill him," the famous exclamation "Mu!" and all the other koans. Koans are not really presented to make us understand how things are, they are just methods for letting go of something we thought is right or wrong, good or bad, something we thought we know, and so on. Given that approach, from a more pessimistic point of view we could say that the Buddhist path is simply one disappointment after the other—the only good thing is that enlightenment is the last one. On a more positive note, we could say that if we go through the intricacies of training the mind in not clinging, it is like training to be a top-notch ballet dancer. When we see those people, their movements seem so light, full of grace, and completely without effort, but actually the training is very hard and they have to pay attention to every minute detail, every day, over and over again. The effortlessness and the lack of rigidity or holding on to anything come only through intense training. Likewise, when we train our mind, nongrasping simply does not happen all by itself out of the blue. For most people, some training is necessary in order to get beyond any need for training.

This means to train in not grasping, not clinging, and not holding on to anything, which is actually much more difficult to accomplish than training in doing something. Doing something is what we are used to and we are very good at it, we are all great overachievers in terms of grasping and clinging. Starting with only very few things as a baby, we keep clinging to more and more, which is what we call our personality, our career, our relationships. All of them just mean to accumulate more and more reference points. However, the path of prajñāpāramitā does the exact opposite, which is why it sometimes seems so difficult, non-sensical, and even scary. We have invested so much in our personality, our career, our relationships, our possessions, and everything else, and then the *Heart Sūtra* tells us, "Just forget about it all." In that way, the prajñāpāramitā sūtras can be like a huge koan collection and even the *Heart Sūtra* is one, with every little phrase of "no this, no that" chipping away at our many-layered cocoon of solidified concepts, emotions, hang-ups, and reference points.

The path of unraveling this cocoon is not a linear one. Usually we think that we start here and then we go there, and a lot of the presentations of the Buddhist path, such as the five paths and ten bhūmis, sound like there is a beginning and then there is a linear progression, with the assumption that all we do on the path is to ascend higher and higher. However, the reality is different—the path is more like the stock market, we go up and down, back and forth, and around. We will revisit the same issues over and over again. That is not really a problem because it is the nature of the Buddhist path. It is not that at some point early on the path we graduate from anger or something like that. Ideally, our anger becomes less frequent and more subtle, but there still can be occasions when it is pretty intense. Then we think, "Oh, man, I meditated for ten years now and I'm still angry! This is not working for me or I must have done something wrong."

We need to understand that when we experience anger, other emotions, illness, or suffering, all of them are results of our former actions and that there are a lot of those results stored in our mind. The path means to empty the big bucket of what is stored in our mind, but as we all know, there is always something stuck in the bottom of the bucket. Also, the fact that all these things are results means that their manifestation is a sign of their going out of our system. Once they have manifested, both they and their causes have ended, which means we are rid of them and they will not come back. However, the crucial point is that we not make these results into new causes for further suffering through repeating or continuing our storyline about them and our negative reactions to them.

In brief, the Buddhist path is more like spiraling toward a middle rather than a straight line from A to B. Of course, if we spiral, we revisit the same spots again and again, but it is never really the same because we see them from a different perspective each time. They may seem the same and so familiar, but if we look closely we see something different every time. The prajñāpāramitā sūtras are meant as contemplative manuals to travel on that spiraling path. That is another reason why they are recited again and again and why they have so many repetitions. Superficially they may all sound the same, but in the spiraling approach of traveling, each time we look at the seemingly same word or spot, it is different. It is like when we read the "same" book five times, we find ourselves learning or experiencing something different every time. It is the same book, but our mind and how it interacts with what it reads is different every time. Likewise, it might be the same sūtra, but when we recite it, it is different every time because our mind is in a different place.

The Commentary on the *Heart Sūtra*

Now let's look at the actual words of the *Heart Sūtra*. My comments are based on all the Indian commentaries on this sūtra as well as several Tibetan and some modern commentaries (for details, see the bibliography). There are basically two different versions of the *Heart Sūtra*. The one that we are using here has a prologue (or an introduction), an epilogue (or a conclusion), and it also contains the mantra of prajñāpāramitā. The other version lacks the introduction and conclusion, and often also lacks the mantra.

The Stage and the Main Actors

The brief structure of the sūtra is that it starts with the introduction or the setting of the sūtra, which tells us where it happened, when it happened, who the teacher was, and who else was there (the usual suspects). In particular, in the *Heart Sūtra* there are two parts to this introduction. There is the common setting of the sūtra, which is found in all prajñāpāramitā sūtras, starting with "Thus have I heard. Once the Bhagavān was residing on Vulture Flock Mountain in Rājagṛha . . ." The uncommon introduction here is that both the Buddha and Avalokiteśvara are resting in samādhi while Śāriputra asks his question. The actual main part of the sūtra consists of the short and the longer answers of Avalokiteśvara, which are followed by the mantra. Finally, there is the conclusion, in which the Buddha basically says to Avalokiteśvara, "Good job!" and then the audience rejoices in what happened.

As we discussed before, this is the only prajñāpāramitā sūtra in which the bodhisattva Avalokiteśvara appears. He not only appears in it, but he is the primary teacher, which is an implicit sign that the teachings on compassion and the path are included in the *Heart Sūtra* too, despite not being mentioned explicitly. So Avalokiteśvara symbolizes the compassion of all buddhas and thereby the entire path that is built on compassion as its fundamental motivation. In Buddhism, compassion means the wish that all sentient beings be free from suffering, which is also the core of bodhicitta. Bodhicitta adds the wish to attain buddhahood in order to be personally able to effectively free sentient beings from suffering. Thus, bodhicitta has two elements—compassion as the mere wish for all sentient beings to be free from suffering and, as a consequence of that wish, striving to attain buddhahood for the sake of all beings. That is, bodhicitta adds the component of making it our personal responsibility to actually free all sentient beings from suffering through becoming a buddha ourselves.

The main goal of bodhisattvas is to free sentient beings from suffering, while the attainment of buddhahood is the means to that end. In other words, buddhahood is more like a by-product of bodhicitta or the bodhisattva path. Usually buddhahood is presented as the final result of the path, which is often understood as being primarily for one's own benefit since it means the relinquishment of all obscurations and the realization of buddha wisdom and its many qualities. However, since the whole point of bodhicitta is to benefit others, the true result of the bodhisattva path is the enlightened activity that a buddha performs for the sake of all beings. And since such activity is only possible on the basis of having become a buddha first, bodhisattvas strive to attain this state. In technical terms, among the three kāyas of a buddha, the dharmakāya represents one's own welfare in terms of supreme relinquishment and realization, which is the formless and dimensionless sphere of a buddha's mind. The welfare of others consists of the two form kāyas—sambhogakāya and nirmāṇakāya—which promote the welfare of both bodhisattvas on the bhūmis and all kinds of ordinary beings, respectively. In brief, like all prajñāpāramitā sūtras, the *Heart*

Sūtra teaches the union of emptiness and skillful conduct (or prajñā and skillful means), with the latter being embodied by Avalokiteśvara.

What are absent from the *Heart Sūtra*, when compared to other prajñāpāramitā sūtras, are any explicit polemics against the foundational Buddhist teachings. There are no disputes between śrāvakas and bodhisattvas, in which the śrāvakas are presented as the ones who don't get it. Still, that element is implicitly represented by Śāriputra, who is the one to ask the question about how to practice prajñāpāramitā.

In general, there are three types of what is called "the word of the Buddha." There are the words that the Buddha himself speaks directly, but there are also "buddha words by blessing" and "buddha words by permission." The *Heart Sūtra* contains all three types. The introduction, which speaks about the setting of the sūtra, is obviously not something that the Buddha himself said, but was added later by the compilers. However, this is still considered the words of the Buddha by permission. The same goes for the epilogue at the end of the sūtra. The main part of the sūtra consists of the words of the Buddha by his blessing. At the beginning of the sūtra the Buddha enters a particular samādhi and it is through the power of that samādhi that Śāriputra pops the question and Avalokiteśvara answers. Therefore, what Avalokiteśvara says is considered as the Buddha's own words, which in the end is confirmed twice by the Buddha, when he says, "Good, good, O son of noble family. Thus it is, O son of noble family, thus it is." These words represent the third type of words by the Buddha, that is, what he says directly. Maybe sometimes the Buddha thought, "This time I let will someone else do the job and I will just give my stamp of approval." Thus, in this sūtra we have all three kinds of what are considered the words of the Buddha—his actual direct speech, speaking through someone else through blessing them, and speaking through someone else by having given them permission.

THE TITLE
Transcendent Wisdom Lady Full of Qualities

The full title of the *Heart Sūtra* is:

The Sūtra of the Heart of the Glorious Lady Prajñāpāramitā.

The Sanskrit *Bhagavatīprajñāpāramitāhṛdayasūtra* literally means "the sūtra of the heart (or the essence) of Bhagavatī Prajñāpāramitā." The meanings of *prajñāpāramitā* and *sūtra* have already been discussed at length above. *Bhagavat* means "possessing fortune," "prosperous," "glorious," "illustrious," "divine," "adorable," or "venerable." In Sanskrit, *prajñāpāramitā* is a feminine word, so the matching feminine word *bhagavatī* means something like "her divine glorious ladyship." Also, in Buddhism wisdom is considered to be female, while compassion or skill in means is regarded as male. Thus, prajñāpāramitā is usually depicted as a female deity, who is also called "the mother of all buddhas." In fact, she is not only the mother of all buddhas, but of all practitioners of the Buddhist paths, traditionally described as "the four kinds of noble ones," which are śrāvakas, pratyekabuddhas, bodhisattvas, and buddhas. Of course, prajñāpāramitā is not the mother of these four in a physical sense, like a human mother and her children. It is the realization of what prajñāpāramitā is—nonconceptual nondual wisdom—that gives rise to the states of mind that are referred to as being an arhat, a bodhisattva, and a buddha.

When we look at what the words of the title of the sūtra mean in more detail, *bhagavat* is a common epithet of the Buddha (as found at the beginning of the *Heart Sūtra*), so Prajñāpāramitā is considered as a female buddha. *Bhaghavat* is often translated as "the blessed one," but besides the meanings mentioned above, the Sanskrit has a lot more connotations. In the commentaries the term is interpreted as having three meanings—"to destroy," "to be endowed," and "to transcend," which are also reflected in the Tibetan translation of the term. What does Prajñāpāramitā destroy? She destroys our obscurations and the activities of māras, which refer to all kinds of external and internal hindrances and obstacles.

Second, she is endowed with six fortunes or six riches. The first one of these is "sovereignty" or "mastery," which refers to having overpowered all obscurations (afflictions and obscurations to omniscience) and being the sole sovereign or mistress of the enlightened mind.

The second fortune is to be "endowed with the dharmas," that is, the qualities of a buddha, such as the ten powers, the four fearlessnesses, and the eighteen unique qualities. From among the five buddha wisdoms, this is nothing other than dharmadhātu wisdom, which represents the fundamental space in which the other four wisdoms play. Here, when we talk about dharmadhātu, it is not just a synonym for mere emptiness, but refers to the nature of our mind, which is the experiential expanse of the union of awareness and emptiness. This nature of our mind is endowed with twofold purity. In itself, it is always intrinsically and naturally pure. However, in terms of the result of buddhahood, there is more to it because buddhahood means that this very nature of our mind is also pure of any adventitious stains that previously seemed to obscure it. Though the nature of the mind is primordially and completely pure, from the perspective of sentient beings who do not realize its purity, at the end of the path it appears that there is an additional purity, in that mind's nature is now both naturally pure and additionally pure of adventitious stains. For example, even if the sun is behind the clouds, in itself it is always unobscured. However, on a grey day, from our perspective below the clouds, it is obscured. Still, this seems to be the case only from our perspective, not from the perspective of the sun itself. Once the clouds disappear we see the sun, and it seems to us that it has become unobscured by clouds. But if we were to ask the sun whether it felt obscured or dimmed down, it would just say, "What are you talking about? I have always been free of clouds. It is your problem if you think that I have been obscured." Likewise, the nature of our mind is always pure by nature, it is without any problems or obscurations, but from the point of view of confusion or ignorance, there first seem to be obscurations and then there seems to be freedom from obscurations, which is the second kind of purity. However, from the point of view of the nature of the mind itself, none of that has ever happened, which is the first kind of purity—natural purity.

The third quality or fortune is "fame," which refers to the two form kāyas of a buddha. The above quality of the double-pure dharmadhātu represents the dharmakāya, which is completely inaccessible to, and cannot be perceived by, anyone but a buddha. "Fame" indicates how the buddhas are known in the world, which is not through the dharmakāya, but through the form kāyas. Among the five wisdoms, this quality corresponds to mirrorlike wisdom.

The fourth fortune or richness is "glory," which refers to the wisdom of equality. The fifth one is "wisdom," which specifically refers to discriminating wisdom. Finally, the sixth one is "effort," which stands for all-accomplishing wisdom.

In brief, the six fortunes or riches of the Bhagavatī Prajñāpāramitā consist of the five wisdoms of a buddha and the freedom from all obscurations (the first fortune). Thus, these six qualities represent an extended version of the two classical qualities of buddhahood—consummate relinquishment and consummate realization, with the latter being divided into the five wisdoms.

Among these five wisdoms, dharmadhātu wisdom is nothing other than the fundamental nature of the mind as it is, which is inseparable spaciousness and luminosity. In the term "dharmadhātu wisdom," "dharmadhātu" stands for mind's quality of infinite spaciousness in which there is nothing to hold on to, while "wisdom" refers to the quality of lucid awareness or wakefulness.

Mirrorlike wisdom means that the wisdom of a buddha is able to see everything very clearly and unmixed. All phenomena are reflected in mirrorlike wisdom just as in a mirror. Similar to a mirror, that wisdom is completely unbiased toward anything that appears in it, nor does it attempt to own anything. It does not think, "This is me," "This is mine," "This is other," "This is good," or "This is bad." Mirrorlike wisdom just shows what is there, it is a panoramic kind of sheer awareness.

The wisdom of equality further highlights the notion of being unbiased. In the wisdom of a buddha there is no me or others, no good or bad, no subject or object. This wisdom also includes not just the cognitive quality of no bias, but also the emotional or affective quality of equality. This means having an equal mind toward all sentient beings, without distinguishing between self and other, or likeable and unlikeable beings. In other words, this translates as nonreferential all-encompassing compassion.

Discriminating wisdom means that though there is no bias with regard to whatever appears in mirrorlike wisdom, there is still a crystal clear discrimination of every detail of every phenomenon. In fact, not being biased is what enables and enhances this sharp clarity of perception, which also shows in our ordinary experience. If we have some fixed biased idea about somebody, as soon as the person comes into sight, we do not even properly look at the details of their appearance, but we zoom down to our own biased mental image of that person, which of course does not really reflect what that person is actually like. By the same token, if we have no biases or rigid ideas about someone or something, we can see clearly what is going on in every situation, and also what is going on in the minds of other sentient beings and what they need. These four wisdoms so far can be summarized into the two categories of knowledge and motivation.

The last one—all-accomplishing wisdom—is what makes buddhas actually do something about all of this. They see everything very clearly and precisely, and without any bias. Because of seeing the equality of self and others, they also see that sentient beings suffer due to ignorance about their true state, which leads buddhas to doing something about this suffering. Therefore, a buddha's wisdom is not just knowing everything about everything and then leaning back and letting the world roll by on its own. It means knowing everything about suffering and happiness, including their causes, having the motivation to benefit others through that knowledge, and also having the power to accomplish that benefit. These three elements have to come together or buddha wisdom is not going to do any good. Merely knowing everything is not helping anybody else. Even if we have the motivation to help other people, that alone does not really help them either, we need to have both knowledge and the means to do so in a powerful and effective way. All three together constitute a buddha, which is what *bhagavat* means—being endowed with all those qualities and also being free of all obscurations and hindrances so that they can manifest.

It is important to understand that the five buddha wisdoms are not five different entities or static qualities of one entity, but stand for the various processes which cooperate with and supplement each other, representing the main functional activities of the single nonconceptual wisdom of a buddha. Mirrorlike wisdom is like an all-encompassing TV screen that simply reflects what is there, thus providing the "raw data" to be processed and used. Discriminating wisdom means to intently look at this screen and clearly see all its distinct data without getting confused or mixing them up. The wisdom of equality refers to being empathic, but lacking any kind of judgment about the data seen on the screen, as well as making no difference between seer and seen. All-accomplishing wisdom represents the resultant impulse to altruistically act upon what is seen.

Thus, nonconceptual buddha wisdom reflects all sentient beings and phenomena within a buddha's field of activity without any bias and personal concern (mirrorlike wisdom). At the same time, this nonconceptual wisdom perceives all these beings and phenomena in every minute detail, just as they are, with perfectly clear discernment and without any personal projections or superimpositions (discriminating wisdom). Nonconceptual wisdom is also completely nondual, which not only refers to its perceptual structure (no subject-object duality), but also to its "emotional intelligence." It neither takes saṃsāra as something bad to be avoided, nor nirvāṇa as something good to dwell in. It lacks any attachment and aversion to anybody or anything, but sees the buddha nature of all beings, which is not different in essence from a buddha's very own state, thus naturally being loving and compassionate toward all those who do not see this (the wisdom of equality). Dharmadhātu wisdom provides the infinite space within which such vast and profound knowing, compassion, and enlightened activity are possible. By virtue of all these features, nonconceptual wisdom is the most efficient mental mode of operation possible. It underlies everything that, from the perspective of those to be benefited, appears as a buddha's helpful activity in an effortless, unpremeditated, and uninterrupted way (all-accomplishing wisdom).

As for the third meaning of *bhagavatī*, the syllable *vān* in *bhagavān* (the masculine nominative) is interpreted as the "vāṇ" in "nirvāṇa." In that sense, *bhagavatī* has the quality of transcendence, specifically the quality of having attained the "nonabiding nirvāṇa," which is the state of being neither in saṃsāra nor in the one-sided nirvāṇa of arhats as one's private peaceful place to hang out. If we are not in either of those two, where are we? We are simply completely lost . . . Seriously, buddhas can be anywhere they want, in as many places as they want, and in as many forms as they want because they are not bound to one location, either physically or mentally. Arhats are still bound to one place, they cannot get back to saṃsāra, but are stuck in their personal little nirvāṇa. This means that they cannot be active for other sentient beings who are still in saṃsāra, whereas buddhas can appear anywhere in saṃsāra or nirvāṇa at any time, there is no obstruction. Therefore, the "nonabiding nirvāṇa" is not the classical nirvāṇa of just attaining liberation for our own benefit. It is much more than that because buddhas are not only free from saṃsāra, but they are still active for the welfare of sentient beings. They are not retreating and enjoying their personal retirement insurance benefits.

Those three meanings of *bhagavatī*—destroying all obscurations, being endowed with all qualities, and going beyond saṃsāra and nirvāṇa—also make up the Tibetan translation (*chomdendé*) of this term. To overcome the two obscurations is the quality of relinquishment. To possess the wisdom dharmakāya is the quality of realization. The quality of transcendence means to be beyond saṃsāra and nirvāṇa and yet be able to appear anywhere in them without being affected by them.

The Heart of the Mother of All Buddhas

The next word in the title is *hṛdaya*, which means "heart" in both a physical and metaphorical sense; the center, core, or essence of something; or the best, dearest, or most secret part of something. So we can say that this sūtra is like the heart of the prajñāpāramitā sūtras, which are like the rest of the body. It is the heart of the matter of the prajñāpāramitā teachings, the teaching on emptiness. The *Heart Sūtra* is the heart essence or the quintessence of all the prajñāpāramitā sūtras, which contains their message in the most distilled form. It teaches the essential meaning of those sūtras briefly and in a very direct manner, but at the same time exhaustively. There is nothing left out—in terms of the essence, we will not find anything in the larger prajñāpāramitā sūtras that is not contained in the *Heart Sūtra*. Therefore, the *Heart Sūtra* is like the heart in our body, which is at its center, is its most essential organ, and also is the one that keeps the whole body alive and functioning. In Asia the heart is also said to be the location of the mind (not the brain, as in the West). That means the heart is where our mind and our emotions are—it is the very center of our existence. In that sense, the *Heart Sūtra* is the very essence or the very core of everything the Buddha had to say.

Among the other prajñāpāramitā sūtras, the one in one hundred thousand lines can be said to resemble the torso; the ones in twenty-five thousand and eighteen thousand lines, the legs; those in ten thousand and eight thousand lines, the arms; the one in two thousand five hundred lines, the head; the verses of the *Prajñāpāramitāsaṃcayagāthā*, the mouth; the *Diamond Cutter Sūtra*, the brain; the remaining ones, feet, hands, toes, and fingers; and the one in a single letter, a single hair on the body.

THE PROLOGUE

The actual text of the sūtra begins with the prologue (or the setting), starting with:

Thus have I heard.

This is the default phrase with which every sūtra starts, which is the introductory remark of the one who recorded the sūtra after having heard it in person. The Buddha's words were not written down for hundreds of years, but were only passed on orally. To people in the age of multimedia and everything being recorded by machines in digital form or hardcopy, this may sound weird and unreliable, but oral transmission of knowledge over many generations has been, and sometimes still is, a very common phenomenon in many societies and cultures around the globe, even after the advent of scripts. For example, in India, for thousands of years the Vedas were not written down at all, but were passed on orally from teacher to student. Not only did people have better memories at those times, but they also had incredibly sophisticated and complex techniques of memorization. For example, even once the Vedas were written down, the students would not just memorize a page line by line from top to bottom, but also backwards from bottom to top and even diagonally. For that purpose they put the words into charts with little boxes, almost like a crossword puzzle, and then they could learn them from any direction. The result of that was a perfect recollection of the entire page. Even if they forgot a word somewhere, they could always come back to it through several of those mnemonic avenues. Oral transmission was the traditional way of preserving the tradition for many thousands of years. Thus, in India at least, it was nothing special, it was completely normal.

As for the words of the Buddha in particular, after his death his followers used to convene at councils at certain times, during which the foremost arhats who were considered experts in a particular aspect of the Buddha's teachings recited what they remembered. The others were listening, occasionally speaking up if they remembered something different, and finally those present agreed on an official version. One of the main arhats who had been entrusted with the words of the Buddha and remembered a lot of them was Ānanda, the Buddha's attendant for many years. In particular, it is said that Ānanda was the one to whom the Buddha entrusted the preservation of the prajñāpāramitā sūtras. In that way, this phrase "Thus have I heard" is an indication of a narrator of a sūtra (such as Ānanda) saying, "This is what I heard from the Buddha and what I am passing on to you." This is how the words of the Buddha were handed down from one person to another. When the teachings were eventually written down, the phrase "Thus have I heard" was retained at the beginning of each sūtra in order to signify this process of an unbroken lineage of transmission.

The Excellent Time

The introduction of the *Heart Sūtra* is said to teach "the five excellencies" in terms of the time, the teacher, the place, the retinue, and the teachings. The excellent time is indicated by "Thus have I heard. Once . . ." Obviously, this is not very specific. The commentaries say that "time" here refers to the time when the virtue in the minds of the audience had ripened to the point that it was possible for the Buddha to give those teachings. Also there are different accounts as to when the prajñāpāramitā sūtras were taught. For example, it is often said that all of them were taught together simultaneously, but that different people in the audience heard different versions, such as those in one hundred thousand, twenty-five thousand, or eight thousand lines, and so on. Others say that some of these sūtras were taught at the same time and others not. Some commentators even say that all the prajñāpāramitā sūtras were taught in a single instant. We can also see in the larger sūtras that, just as today during a longer course of teachings, new people kept coming into the audience. For example, the Buddha started teaching for the original audience, which may have consisted of humans, and then suddenly some gods showed up who also wanted to listen. So the Buddha basically started all over again, but in a different style, explaining the same topic from a different angle.

In Sanskrit, "Thus have I heard" reads *evaṃ mayā śrutam*. The word *evam* is a very important one in the Buddhist teachings on all levels. Literally, it just means "thus." However, its two syllables *e* and *vam* are said to represent the root syllables of all the teachings of the Buddha. They are like the parents of all the letters in the sūtras, the father and the mother of all the eighty-four thousand dharmas that the Buddha taught. Also, *e* and *vam* are said to symbolize prajñā and skill in means, respectively. Or *e* stands for emptiness and *vam*, for compassion, which are the two major principles that, from the mahāyāna point of view, summarize all the teachings of the Buddha.

The Excellent Teacher

The excellent teacher of the *Heart Sūtra* is

the Bhagavān.

The teacher here is not any ordinary instructor or lecturer, but Buddha Śākyamuni, a fully awakened being who possesses all the qualities that were explained above in terms of the Bhagavatī Prajñāpāramitā—having relinquished all obscurations, being endowed with the five wisdoms, and having transcended saṃsāra and nirvāṇa.

Question: The teachings on the paths and bhūmis tend to be very detailed. It has never been clear to me whether all of these teachings are actually included in the sūtras somewhere or whether they are the imagination of the commentators?

KB: That is an interesting question. I would say it depends on your view. A lot of things that we find in the commentaries on the paths and bhūmis are not found explicitly in the sūtras. For example, the prajñāpāramitā sūtras have different names for some of the five paths and the names of the ten bhūmis are not even mentioned in any of these sūtras, nor do they describe them. There is also no systematic description of the five paths in these sūtras in their usual order, starting with the path of accumulation. There are bits and pieces of the sūtras all over the place that are taken as descriptions of these paths by commentators. Sometimes they just take a single word in the sūtra and say that this describes, for example, the path of seeing, which somebody like me would never have guessed. So, on a superficial reading of the prajñāpāramitā sūtras or from the point of view of an ordinary being, we can say that a lot of the teachings on paths and bhūmis that these sūtras supposedly contain were made up by later people. On the other hand, it seems that this also depends on how deeply we understand the meaning of what the Buddha was teaching at the time and what he might have been referring to implicitly or in a hidden manner, which may have triggered different things in the minds of different people. Of course, it is not that the Buddha never taught about the five paths, the ten bhūmis, and so on, we have a lot about them in other sūtras, but in the prajñāpāramitā sūtras themselves the topic of paths and bhūmis is not obvious at all.

That is why this topic is called "the hidden meaning" of the prajñāpāramitā sūtras and it is for the same reason that Maitreya composed his *Ornament of Clear Realization*, the meaning of which is still quite hidden, but it is at least a little bit clearer in terms of the actual paths and bhūmis. Maitreya usually just presents certain key phrases from the sūtras, but we still need the commentaries to flesh out the exact meanings and the full implications of these phrases. Many parts of *The Ornament of Clear Realization* are not obvious at all. Often it lists just one word within fifty or one hundred pages in the sūtras and the next word is found another fifty or one hundred pages later. So the text is more like an extremely condensed form of *Reader's Digest* in terms of the prajñāpāramitā sūtras. Of course, if we try to read it on its own without the context of the sūtras, it does not make any sense, so we need both the sūtras and the commentaries to tell us what it means. But then we also get a lot of different interpretations in different commentaries, sometimes even the opposite. So we can see that the whole enterprise of laying out the five paths and the ten bhūmis is very fluid and evanescent. In itself this is an excellent teaching on emptiness, which is after all what we are supposed to realize on these paths and bhūmis. In other words, we should not solidify all these descriptions of paths and bhūmis or take them too seriously as just being one way and not any other way. Otherwise we are back to square one—we are replacing our being stuck in our ordinary and convoluted saṃsāric paths and bhūmis with being stuck in some equally rigid model of some paths and bhūmis that supposedly free us from the former. These teachings on how to realize emptiness are intended to make our mind more flexible, open, spacious, and relaxed and to break up our solidified concepts, and they were not presented in order to give us even more headaches.

Question: Could you talk a little about the use of a mantra like the prajñāpāramitā mantra and how reciting OM GATE GATE PĀRAGATE PĀRASAMGATE BODHI SVĀHĀ can be used in meditation?

KB: The mantra is basically the heart of the *Heart Sūtra*, whose entire meaning is said to be condensed in this mantra. So when we recite the mantra, we are replaying the *Heart Sūtra* in a very brief form. Also, the mantra is said to reflect the five paths, but we will get to the details later. In essence when we recite the mantra, it provides a focus for our mind in terms of emptiness. Literally it means something like, "Gone, gone, gone beyond, completely gone beyond, may there be enlightenment." It is sometimes said that this mantra was first uttered by Avalokiteśvara at the end of his answer to Śāriputra in this sūtra, which seems to have been the moment when he let go completely. He went over the cliff, he was gone, gone beyond, completely gone beyond any reference points, having let go of everything that we know and are. In this sense the mantra is not only a reminder of that, but actually a gate for us to connect with that experience of completely letting go and, as Milarepa sings in one of his songs, "go where no mind goes." In this way the first part of the mantra is like the path and *BODHI SVĀHĀ* is the fruition. Fundamentally speaking, we could say that the mantra is a reminder and a friendly encouragement to let go (as opposed to other such encouragements that may not be so friendly).

The Excellent Place

Among the five excellencies, the third one is the excellent place, which is

on Vulture Flock Mountain in Rājagṛha.

Most translations of the *Heart Sūtra* render the Sanskrit words *gridhrakūṭa parvata* as "Vulture Peak Mountain." However, *kūṭa* can mean both "peak" and "flock." The commentaries usually explain it to mean the latter, which is also reflected in the Tibetan translation using the word "heap" or "group" (*phungpo*) instead of "peak." Thus, *gridhrakūṭa* means a flock of vultures. According to some commentaries, the mountain received its name from the shape of its rock formations that resemble a flock of vultures huddled together, which you can actually see when you are there. Others say that the entire mountain looks like a vulture. Some hold that the name comes from the flocks of vultures that usually land on top of that mountain and are actually beings who understand emptiness. Yet others say that it is due to vultures protecting the mountain, on which many such birds feed on corpses. Another explanation is that when the Buddha was teaching there, his robes were snatched by a demon in the form of a vulture and then dropped on the mountain, where they turned into stone in four layers. No matter which of these interpretations we prefer, the place where all the prajñāpāramitā sūtras were taught is considered to be a special one.

The Excellent Retinue

Fourth, the excellent retinue consists of

> a great assembly of fully ordained monks and a great assembly
> of bodhisattvas.

As we can see from the epilogue of the *Heart Sūtra*, there were a lot of beings in the audience, including gods, demigods, and all kinds of fairies, so the two types of saṅgha explicitly mentioned here point to the most eminent persons in the audience. Here the "assembly of fully ordained monks (*bhikṣus*)" refers to the entire ordained saṅgha of the foundational approach of Buddhism, that is, novices as well as fully ordained monks and nuns. The "great assembly of bodhisattvas" is mentioned separately not only in order to distinguish the saṅgha of the followers of the mahāyāna, but also because bodhisattvas can either be monastic or not, and as we can see in the sūtras, a lot of them are actually lay practitioners. In terms of the foundational Buddhist approach, being a monastic is strongly emphasized as the ideal of the Buddhist practitioner. It is always clearly said that as long as we are not a monastic, we cannot really practice properly. The role of the lay Buddhists is primarily to practice generosity for the monastic community, which is still the traditional setting in Asian Buddhist countries. By contrast, in the mahāyāna the bodhisattva path is open to everybody and can be practiced by both monastics and nonmonastics, either male of female. Originally monasticism was not so strongly emphasized in the mahāyāna teachings, though that changed later.

Thus the human audience of the *Heart Sūtra* consisted of the saṅghas of śrāvakas, pratyekabuddhas, and bodhisattvas. The śrāvakas are called "hearers" because they hear the teachings from the Buddha or some other teacher and then proclaim them to others, thus making those others also hear the words of the Buddha. The pratyekabuddhas are "solitary buddhas" or "self-made buddhas" because they achieve their fruition without a teacher. For a period of one hundred eons they rely on teachers and listen to their instructions, studying and practicing in the same way as the śrāvakas. However, in their last life in which they achieve the arhathood of a pratyekabuddha, by virtue of their previous

aspiration prayers they are born in a situation where there are no buddhas. At that point they do not have a teacher, but due to their former
training, when they see a bone or a skeleton, that immediately triggers
the whole chain of the twelve links of dependent origination in reverse
order in them. That is, upon seeing a bone, they immediately think, "Oh,
yeah, that comes from death, and death comes from aging, which comes
from birth, which stems from becoming and grasping" and so on. In
this way, they go back through the twelve links all the way down to ignorance. Thus, their main meditation is on the twelve links of dependent
origination. There are two types of pratyekabuddhas. The "rhinoceros-
like" ones prefer to stay and practice alone; they are the typical solitary
buddhas who do not mingle with anybody. The second ones are of
the "parrot" type and practice together in small groups in forests and
other solitary places. Also, pratyekabuddhas usually do not teach others
through words, but through performing miraculous feats, which create
inspiration for the dharma in other people.

Bodhisattvas are those who practice the mahāyāna teachings of the
Buddha. If we break down the word *bodhisattva*, *bodhi* means "enlightenment," "realization," or "awakening" and *sattva* can mean "being,"
"mind," or "courageous." That is why some people call bodhisattvas
"enlightenment heroes or warriors." In brief, bodhisattvas are beings who
strive for enlightenment or who have enlightenment in their mind, having
generated bodhicitta, the mind of enlightenment. We could also say that
they are those who are courageous enough to strive for enlightenment.
Why do they need courage for that? Bodhisattvas are not afraid of three
things—the infinite number of sentient beings they are supposed to lead
to enlightenment (since they took the bodhisattva vow), the infinite time it
takes to bring them to enlightenment, and the infinite hardships they have
to go through in order to do all that (both to become buddhas themselves
and to work with other, often difficult, sentient beings). As we all know, it
is not always a joy ride when we try to help people.

In the introductions to the larger prajñāpāramitā sūtras there are
usually more extensive descriptions of the setting, such as describing all
the qualities that the śrāvakas, pratyekabuddhas, and bodhisattvas present possess. These sūtras also describe at length what the Buddha did

before he actually started teaching verbally, such as extensive displays of his miraculous powers (radiating light throughout the universe and so on). However, we do not have to deal with those descriptions here because this is the *Heart Sūtra*.

The Excellent Teaching

Fifth, the excellent teaching is identified in the special prologue of the *Heart Sūtra*. Its common introduction (or prologue), which is—in more or less great detail—common to all prajñāpāramitā sūtras, ends with "a great assembly of bodhisattvas." The next sentence identifies the excellent teaching:

> At that time the Bhagavān entered the samādhi of the enumerations of phenomena called "perception of the profound."

The Buddha entered this special samādhi and it is out of that meditative state or inspirational background that the whole *Heart Sūtra* unfolds. Thus the teaching of the sūtra comes directly out of the mind of the Buddha in meditation. As for "the samādhi of the enumerations of phenomena called 'perception of the profound,'" most commentaries make it clear that among the many different meanings of "dharma," here the term does not have the sense of the Buddha's teaching, but refers to phenomena. The word *dharma* comes from the root *dhṛ* ("to hold"). Thus, conventionally speaking, a phenomenon is what holds or bears its own nature. For example, the nature of fire is to be hot and burning. This is what we call a phenomenon—something that bears a nature that is distinct from other phenomena. "Enumerations" refers to the different types of phenomena, which are the well-known Buddhist categories of skandhas, dhātus, āyatanas, and so on (for details on these, see below).

What does "perception of the profound" mean? It can mean a lot of things, depending on how we read the Sanskrit words *gambhīrāvasaṃbodha* or *gambhīrāvabhāsa* in different versions of the sūtra. *Gambhīra* means "profound." *Avasaṃbodha* means "perfect knowledge or understanding," "awakening," "perceiving," "observing," and "recognizing," while *avabhāsa* means "light," "appearance," "manifestation," and "seeing" (which corresponds to the Tibetan translation *nangwa*). Thus this samādhi refers to the perception or illumination of what is profound—it is not so much that the perception or illumination itself is profound, but that which is perceived or illuminated, which is emptiness, the profound nature of phenomena. The perception in this samādhi consists of the nonconceptual nondual wisdom that realizes profound emptiness. This wisdom is the only kind of perception for which something so profound and difficult to realize as emptiness can actually appear in an immediate manner. For example, it is not difficult for the reflections of the sun, the moon, and the stars to appear in a lake, but it is difficult for the entirety of space to its very limits to be reflected in that lake. Likewise, it is easy to perceive the phenomena of conventional reality, but it is difficult to perceive the ultimate reality that is emptiness.

The way in which nonconceptual wisdom illuminates emptiness is illustrated in one commentary by the example of blowing air into a fire, which makes the fire blaze brighter and thus illuminates things, making them clearly visible. Likewise, this samādhi is like blowing air into the fire of prajñā and thus making emptiness perceptible for the audience. Through the power of that samādhi, the audience gets at least a glimpse of what emptiness is. Another way to understand this is that the profound light of this samādhi illuminates the darkness of ignorance. In brief, this samādhi illuminates or perceives all the different types of phenomena that are presented in the Buddhist teachings by way of illuminating or perceiving what is profound about them, which is emptiness. This means that those phenomena themselves are illuminated or perceived as being illusionlike—appearing, yet ultimately unfindable and unreal.

One commentary also says that the two phrases "perception of the profound" (that is, perceiving profound emptiness) and "enumerations of phenomena" (that is, perceiving all the types of phenomena) refer to the two types of buddha wisdom. The former represents "the wisdom of suchness," which realizes how things truly are. The latter is "the wisdom of variety," which refers to knowing all phenomena in their distinct ways of appearing and interacting. These two types of wisdom enable buddhas not only to know the actual ultimate nature of all phenomena, but also to deal with the complex and confused worlds of sentient beings. If buddhas only rested in how things truly are all the time, it would be impossible for them to make any connection, or interact, with deluded sentient beings who perceive all kinds of phenomena except how things truly are. As the *Heart Sūtra* says, "In emptiness there is no form, no feeling . . ." If buddhas just perceive that emptiness without any forms and so on, how will they interact with sentient beings who have, perceive, and cling to forms, feelings, and so on?

However, it is said that "the wisdom of variety" does not refer to what buddhas actually perceive from the perspective of their own minds because all their obscurations—ordinary phenomena such as skandhas, dhātus, and āyatanas—are gone. Rather, this wisdom is a little bit similar to when we watch something on a TV screen. We can clearly see very faraway places on that screen, such as Afghanistan, and we can see what is going on there, such as when we watch the news (not CNN or Fox "News," but real news, such as the British BBC). But watching what is going on in, for example, the war in Afghanistan does not mean that we are actually in the middle of this war to experience it with all its atrocities—we do not get shot or bombed if we watch that war on TV. Still, we can see all the details of what is happening there, we react to it emotionally (such as, ideally, feeling compassion for all the victims as well as the attackers), and we can also do something about it (such as sending money to Doctors Without Borders and making petitions to end this war).

In this "samādhi of the perception of the profound" the Buddha is absorbed or resting in the nature of the mind, which is also known as buddha nature. The power of that samādhi has an effect on the audience in that the Buddha kindles the energy of his own buddha nature to radiate out to the audience, which triggers a reaction in the buddha nature of everybody present. To use a somewhat crude example, if we pluck a string on a single violin among an assembly of violins, the corresponding strings on all the other violins will also start resounding, without even touching them. Here the Buddha is playing the full symphony of buddha nature, so to speak, and the buddha natures of everyone in the audience chime in as best as they can.

Furthermore, it is said that the only reason for the Buddha entering this samādhi at the beginning of the *Heart Sūtra* was his compassion.

From his own side, the Buddha has no need to enter into any kind of samādhi because buddhas dwell in the nature of phenomena all the time anyway. For them, there is no separation between being in meditation and not being in meditation. Thus, when the Buddha entered that samādhi, it was basically for pedagogic purposes, that is, in order to instruct others. What this samādhi does is to mature the mind streams of the audience so that the "content" or the experiential sphere of that samādhi—the profound nature of phenomena—can be perceived by them too. This samādhi represents an immediate and direct form of mind-to-mind transmission, which is shown by Avalokiteśvara being in samādhi too. Thus, we could say that there are at least two levels of communication here in the *Heart Sūtra*. The more obvious one is that Śāriputra is asking and Avalokiteśvara is answering, while the rest of the audience is listening. However, the ultimate power source of that discourse is the Buddha's samādhi. It is that which actually brings it to life in the minds of the audience. Therefore, what Śāriputra asks and what Avalokiteśvara answers are nothing but the natural outflow or resonance of that samādhi. Their dialogue is the skillful means, but its source is the mind of the Buddha. To use another crude example, Avalokiteśvara is like a radio and his entering samādhi is like being plugged in, while the Buddha's samādhi is like a news broadcaster being broadcast. With the broadcast and the plugged-in radio, the audience can listen to what the news broadcaster has to say.

Avalokiteśvara—Emptiness with a Heart of Compassion

This brings us to Avalokiteśvara and what he was doing while the Buddha was in samādhi. The sūtra says:

> At the same time noble Avalokiteśvara, the bodhisattva mahāsattva, while practicing the profound prajñāpāramitā, saw the following: he saw the five skandhas to be empty of nature.

Thus, the most immediate beneficiary of the Buddha's samādhi was Avalokiteśvara, being the closest one to the power source. When the

Buddha entered his samādhi, Avalokiteśvara tuned in and saw the five skandhas to be empty of nature. He essentially saw what the Buddha saw. Who is this person Avalokiteśvara? He was one of the eight foremost bodhisattvas during the time of the Buddha and is seen as the embodiment of the compassion of all buddhas, just as Mañjuśrī is the embodiment of their wisdom. Avalokiteśvara literally means "the mighty one (*īśvara*) who looks down (*avalokita*)." Avalokiteśvara does not look down on us in the negative sense of that expression, but he is looking down on us suffering beings in saṃsāra from his abode beyond saṃsāra with his tremendously compassionate eyes. His compassion is not ordinary, but nonreferential and encompassing all beings in an unbiased way, which is the highest form of compassion that we can have.

Generally, Buddhism speaks about three types of compassion, each increasingly more subtle and at the same time more powerful. The first one is the compassion of ordinary beings as we know it, which focuses on sentient beings who suffer. In this compassion there is a clear sense of distinguishing between someone who has compassion, someone who is the object of that compassion, and the mental engagement of having compassion. We can also further develop this kind of compassion through mind training techniques (*lojong*), such as *tonglen*, or other methods for systematically cultivating compassion in the Buddhist tradition. Then it becomes a more "organized" form of compassion, a type of meditation. This is referred to as "the samādhi of focusing on sentient beings as those who strive for happiness and wish to be free of suffering." At that point, we are not just aware that there are sentient beings out there, but we are very clearly aware that they actually suffer despite seeking for nothing but happiness. Therefore, we wish that they will be free from suffering, which is the Buddhist definition of compassion. Of course, this kind of compassion is still coarse and dualistic, there is a clear sense of subject-object separation and interaction. It can even be somewhat fishy, such as us feeling like the better or superior persons who have compassion for those who are in such worse situations below us, who are the recipients of our compassion.

The second and deeper type of compassion is "the compassion that focuses on the dharma." This means to have realized that sentient beings lack a personal self and then to focus on them as beings who are characterized by not having a real self (which includes ourselves). So this type of compassion focuses on sentient beings as deluded beings who suffer because they think they have a self, whereas they do not. In that way, the compassion that focuses on the dharma means that we are focusing more on the primary cause of suffering, which is ego-clinging. We develop compassion here because of seeing that sentient beings unnecessarily suffer due to their fundamental misperception of who they are and of how to attain true happiness. Therefore, this type of compassion is not just the wish for sentient beings to be free of suffering, but it is also the wish for them to be free of the main cause of suffering—clinging to a self.

The third type of compassion is nonreferential compassion, which means to have realized that sentient beings not only lack a personal self, but do not really exist altogether. In other words, this is the compassion that is based on the realization of the emptiness of all phenomena, so we focus on sentient beings as those who are characterized by the lack of real existence—they are just illusory appearances. At first glance, that might sound self-contradictory—if there is nobody, on whom are we focusing and for whom do we have compassion? Also, if there is no one to do the focusing or have compassion, what are we talking about? Though great bodhisattvas see very clearly that there are no real sentient beings or bodhisattvas anywhere, sentient beings themselves do not see that and thus suffer. So the compassion of such bodhisattvas is again due to seeing sentient beings suffer by virtue of a misperception, which here is even deeper than the one under the second type of compassion—the misperception of illusory sentient beings that they and their suffering do really exist. Not only do beings lack a personal self, but also their skandhas, to which they cling as "me" and what is mine, do not really exist either. Therefore, the realization of what is the fundamental cause of suffering is even more profound here—there is nothing to hold on to, and any attempt that we make to try to hold on to anything is what creates our suffering. Seeing that beings suffer because of not realizing that gives rise to all-encompassing but nonsolidifying compassion as the wish to liberate these illusory beings from their illusory error and all its illusory consequences.

The first type of compassion obviously exists in all ordinary beings to a greater or lesser degree. One does not have to be a Buddhist to have that kind of compassion—sometimes it even seems to help not to be a Buddhist. The second compassion, of focusing on the dharma in terms of understanding that sentient beings have no self, exists from the śrāvaka path of accumulation onward. Once we have entered the śrāvaka path and we achieve some understanding that beings actually do not have any personal self, our compassion is deepened by that understanding. The third type of compassion in its actual form only exists from the first bhūmi of bodhisattvas onward, but there is a semblance of it on the mahāyāna path in general even before the first bhūmi.

With the first type of compassion we assume that sentient beings are real, we are real, suffering is real, and we want real sentient beings to really be free of real suffering, so it is all very serious and heavy-handed. There is nothing wrong with this kind of compassion; in fact it is very necessary for beginners on the path. However, from the ultimate Buddhist point of view, this compassion is very limited in both its scope and power—it is still way too rigid. For ultimately the most fundamental cause of suffering is this big misunderstanding of taking persons and phenomena as something that they are not. There are no real persons and there is no real suffering. The more we understand that, the more mental freedom we have, and conversely, the more we solidify ourselves, other sentient beings, and suffering, the more limited our compassion is.

Usually we think it is the other way around—we really suffer and they really suffer, we can feel it so intensely, it is all so terrible and depressing, and only then can we start to feel some real compassion. We just need to watch the daily news with one disaster after the other and we are completely overwhelmed by the continuous avalanche of world-wide suffering. But when we reify and solidify all this and lack a wider view, there is no spaciousness in our compassion, it is very claustrophobic and heavy. At the same time, in the mahāyāna we are supposed to extend our compassion to all sentient beings, not just a few. But if we take our own suffering and the suffering of all these beings very seriously, it is not very likely that we can extend our compassion beyond a handful of beings because their real suffering becomes too overwhelming and we cannot bear it. If we think of all the real and solid suffering of all those real solid beings who are infinite in number, it is too much. Therefore, to wholeheartedly apply our compassion to all beings and to still be able to do something about it as a bodhisattva only works if we have a light touch and lots of space in our approach, which comes through studying, reflecting on, meditating on, experiencing, and eventually realizing emptiness. This is the reason why bodhisattvas are able to remain in saṃsāra forever without being affected by it in the slightest. If we take ourselves, other beings, and all their suffering as really existent, it is completely crazy to even think about taking the bodhisattva vow. How could we as a single really existent sentient being ever eliminate the really existent suffering of limitless really existent beings? This is a more than daunting task for a single ordinary being, so something has to shift here, which is our outlook on the whole enterprise.

Compassion in Action

The second part of Avalokiteśvara's name means "mighty" (*īśvara*). He is mighty because he is truly able to eliminate the suffering of beings. Bodhisattvas not only have good motivation in the form of those three types of compassion, but they are also able to translate their compassion into beneficial actions. Iconographically, there are several forms of Avalokiteśvara, with four arms and even one thousand arms and eleven heads. This illustrates that Avalokiteśvara's compassion does not just consist of some kind of silent wish or some good intentions (as we know, those are what the road to hell is paved with), but it means compassion in constant action.

There is a story about when Avalokiteśvara still had only two hands and one head and he was busily trying to empty the hell realms all by himself, taking the bodhisattva vow very seriously. He was working like mad to empty the hell realms and finally, believe it or not, he actually succeeded. So he turned around for just a moment to take a break and a deep breath and when he turned back, the hell realms were as full as before he had started. At that point Avalokiteśvara experienced a little dent in his bodhicitta, he slipped into a motivational crisis. Then Amitabha appeared to him and said, "Don't worry, from now on I will give you more hands and heads." He gave him one thousand hands with an eye in each hand and also ten more heads (including Amitabha's own head) to be able to see and do more and thus be more efficient. This story shows that, given the infinite number of beings, it is very hard to ever really empty saṃsāra. Still, bodhisattvas have exactly that motivation, but they are only able to really go through with it if things are not solid because otherwise they would just go crazy or become burned-out, helpless helpers.

Of course this does not mean that the bodhisattva vow and bodhisattva activity are just some kind of game, because for sentient beings suffering is not a game, but something to be urgently addressed. Nevertheless, for bodhisattvas the whole thing is much more lighthearted because they see the illusory quality of it all. This also means that the suffering of others does not really make bodhisattvas suffer in terms of their own experience, whereas we usually feel we are not really compassionate if we do not at least suffer a little bit with the ones whom we see suffering. True compassion does not mean that those who feel compassion have to suffer too. Actually, it is said that when bodhisattvas see someone suffer, in terms of their own experience they are delighted because they have a chance to help somebody, which is simply what they like doing best and all of the time. They are of course not delighted about the suffering of some being, but they are delighted because they wish and are able to actually do something about it. This is a little bit similar to what a skilled physician who truly loves his job, versus a person with no medical training, feels when happening upon an injured person. The physician is delighted and immediately starts to work on taking care of the patient, while the other person most probably feels overwhelmed and might even freak out or faint.

In the sūtra Avalokiteśvara is also called "noble." In Buddhism this refers to persons who, in terms of the five paths, are on the path of seeing and above. That is, all śrāvakas, pratyekabuddhas, and bodhisattvas on their respective paths of seeing and upward are called "noble ones" because they have seen true reality directly. Everybody below those paths is called an "ordinary being." In particular, Avalokiteśvara's being referred to as a noble one means that, as a bodhisattva on the tenth bhūmi, he is free of the two obscurations (afflictive and cognitive obscurations). In addition, Avalokiteśvara is not only a bodhisattva but also a "mahāsattva." A mahāsattva literally means somebody who is endowed with a great mind. Thus, mahāsattvas are those whose minds are vast enough to aim at becoming the highest among all beings—a buddha—and who then work to establish everybody else in that state too. In one of the prajñāpāramitā sūtras Śāriputra says that bodhisattvas are called "mahāsattvas" because they teach the dharma in order to relinquish great wrong views, such as clinging to a self, existence, nonexistence, permanence, and extinction. Subhūti declares that bodhisattvas are mahāsattvas because they are not attached to anything on the bodhisattva path (including bodhicitta and the omniscience of a buddha) nor to anything among the paths and fruitions of śrāvakas and pratyeka-buddhas, no matter how nice those paths may be. According to the commentator Haribhadra, the reasons for calling great bodhisattvas such as Avalokiteśvara both "bodhisattva" and "mahāsattva" are as follows. In a general sense, "bodhisattvas" are those whose minds (sattva) or intentions are directed toward the accomplishment of their own welfare, that is, enlightenment (bodhi) as not clinging to any phenomena. However, it may be said that śrāvakas can also be like that. Therefore, one speaks of "mahāsattvas." Secondly, those whose minds are directed toward the accomplishment of the welfare of others are mahāsattvas, but it may be said that altruistic people among non-Buddhists can also be mahāsattvas in that sense. Therefore, the word "bodhisattva" is used too.

Not Seeing the World as We Know It

As mentioned before, through the blessing of the Buddha's samādhi Avalokiteśvara also entered samādhi, which is expressed here as

> while practicing the profound prajñāpāramitā.

This means that Avalokiteśvara, like all bodhisattvas on the path, practiced the enlightening conduct of the six pāramitās while abiding in the realization of the dharmadhātu, or emptiness. Thus he engaged in the equality of such realization while in meditative equipoise, and in the conduct outside of formal meditation which is supported and pervaded by that realization. In this way, bodhisattvas engage in the union of prajñā and skillful means, or the two accumulations of merit and wisdom. They do so through the ten dharma activities of writing the letters of the dharma, venerating both it and those who proclaim it, practicing generosity for both of these, listening to the dharma, reading it, memorizing it, explaining it to others, reciting it, reflecting on it, and meditating on it.

While being engaged in such practice, the sūtra says Avalokiteśvara "saw" something, that is,

he saw the five skandhas to be empty of nature.

This means that he saw that all phenomena neither arise nor cease, they never really come into existence in the first place nor do they go out of existence later. This is just like in an illusion or a movie. A person in a movie is fundamentally unarisen. Such a person has no parents, was never born, and does not have any birth certificate or ID. The person seems to appear, do certain things, and then cease at some point. However, in actual fact, there was no person ever in a movie who arose or was born, and even if that person dies in the movie, they do not really die. The only place where they appear and die is in our mind, in the mind of the watcher. Other than that, the movie characters just consist of moving light dots on a screen onto which we project all our usual projections, such as these characters having been born, doing certain things, feeling certain emotions, thinking certain thoughts, and dying in certain ways. Avalokiteśvara sees through all of this, seeing that the five skandhas do not arise, do not cease, are empty of subject and object, and are generally empty of any nature of their own.

In general, it is said there are three different ways in which the five skandhas are viewed. Ordinary beings see the skandhas as being a person, a self, or a sentient being. When we see somebody coming through the door, we say, "This is Jean" or "That is John." However, all we see is some moving shape and color, which we treat as a person. Of course that is not all there is to a person because there is the mind of that person, which we cannot perceive. The only things that we can actually perceive of a person are what our senses tell us, while the rest is a complete imputation on our part. We cannot perceive anything that goes on in the mind of that person. We only make assumptions and judgments based on outer signs in terms of their body and speech as well as our own moods and preconceptions. When we see somebody coming in the door and we label them as "Jean" or "John," we can see already how much we superimpose on merely a visual perception. It is also clear that the degree of our superimpositions is based on our previous experiences and our state of emotional preoccupation with what we perceive. If we see somebody coming in whom we have known for a long time, immediately there is a whole complex of superimpositions based on the past, such as considering this person as a friend (a pleasant and attractive object) or someone whom we do not like and want to avoid (an unpleasant object). On the other hand, if we just look at this cushion, nothing like that happens—it is a much more neutral object. We also superimpose things onto the cushion, such as it being blue, round, and out there, but usually there is not that much intensity around that (unless it is our own precious cushion being used by someone else). We have much more going on regarding what we perceive as persons. Also, our reactions to and our interactions with those persons are based on our preceding sense perceptions, but to an even greater degree, imputing what the person might think, feel, react, and so on.

This is the view that ordinary beings have about the five skandhas, which not only applies to the skandhas of others, but also to our own, except that we can see our own mind to some extent. We can notice our own mental skandhas, not just our body, and it is mainly due to our noticing our own mental skandhas that we think we know what is going on in the minds of other people. For when we have a certain emotion or thought, we often have a corresponding physical and/or verbal reaction or expression that is triggered by what is going on in our mind. If we spot the physical or verbal expression of someone else that looks similar to our own when we feel a certain way, we immediately assume that this person must have the same feeling or the same thought. Sometimes we are right and sometimes we are not, and this is what we call "communication." It works sometimes, but even if it works, it only does so because of that built-in assumption on both sides, because both sides make the same systemic mistake of projecting onto others.

Therefore, it can be very hard to communicate with people who do not play that game, such as realized beings. Their way of communication is either very different or it simply does not happen in the way that we are used to. From that point of view, what we call "communication" is nothing but a common agreement on the same screw-up, which is mutual projection and assigning certain meanings to certain sounds that we call "language." Thus, both verbal and nonverbal communication work within the parameters of our conceptual mind imputing meaning onto the visual forms, sounds, smells, tastes, and tangible objects that our senses perceive. Then we create even further conceptual imputations onto the concepts that derived from the original sense perceptions. Of course what we are doing here right now is no exception to that.

How do śrāvakas and pratyekabuddhas see the five skandhas? They do not really see the five skandhas as sentient beings or real persons because they understand that there is no personal self. From our ordinary perspective, they have a somewhat more depressing view of the skandhas because they see them as the first two noble truths—the truths of suffering and the origin of suffering. For them that is all that sentient beings are—the five skandhas without a self, which consist of the three types of suffering and the causes for further suffering (afflictions and karmic actions).

Bodhisattvas see the five skandhas as being empty of any inherent existence, being just like illusions, movies, or dreams. However, at the same time, bodhisattvas are very aware that, from the perspective of those sentient beings who cling to their skandhas as being really existent and having a self, their suffering is completely real and the causes for this suffering are also completely real, which is the reason why they suffer. Therefore, the outlook of bodhisattvas is twofold. In terms of their own realization or wisdom, they see that sentient beings are illusionlike, but that is only one side of the coin. The other side of the coin is compassion. Sentient beings suffer precisely because they do not realize that their skandhas are not real, so they keep grasping at illusory and fleeting phenomena. Bodhisattvas see clearly that this is the cause of sentient beings' suffering and thus spontaneously feel compassion toward them, wishing to relieve them from their erroneous and self-destructive views and behaviors.

As the Dalai Lama said many times, the "altruistic logic" of a bodhisattva is not personal, but it is much more powerful in terms of actually eliminating suffering. When bodhisattvas see suffering they do not ask, "Whose suffering is this?" They do not distinguish between "my suffering," "your suffering," or "their suffering." Suffering is just suffering, and suffering is something that always needs to be eliminated, no matter whose it is or in what form it appears. Thus, whenever bodhisattvas see suffering, they do not take it personally as we do and make a lot of fuss about it; their main focus is simply how to get rid of it. By contrast, our own outlook on suffering is extremely personal and we usually just make it worse by fussing a lot even about little things that annoy us. In addition, we distinguish between our own suffering and the suffering of other beings, always taking our own suffering to be much worse, no matter what it is. Bodhisattvas have a more equal outlook on suffering, in that it does not really matter who is suffering—as long as it is suffering, it is to be removed. That is the logic of bodhisattvas, which is based on not differentiating between ourselves and others and also on having realized that there is no true person or self within the skandhas that is "the sufferer."

This concludes the introduction, or the prologue, of the sūtra.

THE MAIN PART OF THE SŪTRA
Śāriputra's Innocent Question

The actual main part of the sūtra consists of Śāriputra's question and Avalokiteśvara's answer. The sūtra says:

> Then, through the power of the Buddha, venerable Śāriputra spoke thus to noble Avalokiteśvara, the bodhisattva mahā-sattva: "How should a son of noble family or a daughter of noble family train who wishes to practice the profound prajñāpāramitā?"

Śāriputra is basically asking Avalokiteśvara, "Tell me, what do you see due to the power of the Buddha's samādhi and what do I need to do to get there?" In other words, Śāriputra wants to know what the path of a bodhisattva consists of and what its fruition is. The sūtra says here explicitly that all that happens in it is "through the power of the Buddha," which refers back to the Buddha's samādhi called "perception of the profound." As for "a son or daughter of noble family," this does not refer to any ordinary family or some kind of mundane aristocracy, but it indicates the spiritual "aristocracy" of bodhisattvas, who are the noble family of the buddhas. The sons and daughters of noble family are bodhisattvas who are born into the family of the buddhas. When we take the bodhisattva vow with the usual formula, at the end we rejoice in having taken the vow with the following words:

Today I am born into the family of the Buddha.
Now I am a child of the Buddha.
From now on I will perform
The actions befitting my family.
I will not be a stain
On this faultless, noble family.

Here "child of the Buddha" refers to the sons or daughters of the Buddha. In general, the Buddha is said to have had three kinds of children. His physical son was Rāhula. The children of his speech are the arhats of śrāvakas and pratyekabuddhas because they achieve their realizations through the speech of the Buddha. The sons and daughters of his mind or heart are the bodhisattvas, who give rise to bodhicitta (the state of mind that is the very heart of enlightenment) and who wish to realize emptiness.

Therefore, once we have taken the bodhisattva vow we are a member of the family of all buddhas because that is the distinctive mark of buddhas, and to act according to this vow is what buddhas do. In a more profound sense, "family" refers to our buddha nature, the fundamental disposition in our mind to become a fully awakened buddha. Generally it is said that people on the Buddhist path have different dispositions, such as tending to follow the śrāvaka path, the pratyekabuddha path, or the bodhisattva path. However, from the mahāyāna point of view, those different dispositions are just temporary differences. Fundamentally all beings have the same disposition or potential to become a buddha, which is called "buddha nature." In other words, this is the basic nature of the mind of all sentient beings. When we become bodhisattvas that nature of the mind is the "family" that we are "born" into, which means that we actively and fully engage in our buddha nature in the way that all buddhas do. We wholeheartedly claim our natural heritage, so to speak.

Once we have joined that family through the bodhisattva vow, we naturally want to learn the "family trade" of engaging in the view, the meditation, the conduct, and the fruition of the bodhisattva path. Therefore, Śāriputra asks how those "who wish to practice the profound prajñāpāramitā" should train. To "practice the profound prajñāpāramitā" means that, at any given moment, we try to connect whatever we do with the profound view of emptiness. At the level of a beginner, this basically means to be more relaxed in whatever we do, have a sense of more space, and not be so claustrophobic, that is, not make everything narrow, super-real, and awfully serious. It also means to have some sense of good-natured humor about ourselves, others, and the whole situation of being on this path. If we can laugh about ourselves and our own situation, that is already a good dose of emptiness because it breaks up the solidity, the seriousness, and the claustrophobic narrow-mindedness of our usual behavior. Anything that contributes to having a lighter touch in our life is a very practical element of emptiness. It does not always have to be this big and lofty concept "emptiness." Sometimes an experience of emptiness can be very simple. Of course, in itself, emptiness is always very simple, but when we see that it is simple, when we break out of our usual solitary confinement of ego-mind, when some light and fresh air come into our musty, gloomy, and complex cocoon of being tied up in our own fetters, that is emptiness, and it feels pretty good.

Usually emptiness does not receive such a good press. Most people, when they hear "emptiness," think of something like an empty bottle, an empty house, an empty wallet, or simply nothingness. But that is not at all what the Buddha meant by emptiness. As a philosophical concept or technical term it refers to all phenomena's lack of any intrinsic nature or their lack of any findable real existence. However, in terms of the experience of emptiness, it means freedom, openness, spaciousness, a lot of fresh air, a lot of space, a lot of lightness, and no one can really complain about that.

Avalokiteśvara's Not So Innocent Short Answer

Avalokiteśvara's short answer to Śāriputra's question about how bodhisattvas should practice prajñāpāramitā is to briefly report what he himself saw in his samādhi that want-to-be bodhisattvas also need to see, referring to both the view and the meditation of the mahāyāna. Therefore, he tells Śāriputra that

> a son of noble family or a daughter of noble family who wishes to practice the profound prajñāpāramitā should see in this way: they see the five skandhas to be empty of nature.

Thus Avalokiteśvara answers Śāriputra's question "What do you do when you practice prajñāpāramitā?" by basically saying, "You don't really do anything." Above we talked about the root of *śūnyatā* being "to swell up," so the five skandhas are like five balloons inflated by egomind. What Avalokiteśvara saw and all bodhisattvas need to see is that the five skandhas are empty of nature, which means to see the hollowness of these balloons and to pop them. More precisely, if we see the illusory nature of an illusion, this does not mean that it disappears, but we are aware that it is not real. For example, if we go to a show with an illusionist such as David Copperfield, once we figure out the trick, whatever appears is not that powerful anymore and it does not exert much control over us anymore. Likewise, if we figure out that the five skandhas are an illusion, we are no longer hypnotized by them. Or when we wake up from a nightmare, we realize that all those frightening things did not really happen and we can relax. This shows what the subjective side of realizing emptiness is. It is not just about seeing things as illusory and so what? The important and liberating thing about emptiness is the difference in how we react to things that we see as solid and really existent versus things that we know are not really real. This reaction is what determines how seriously we take things and whether we suffer from them or not. The more seriously we take things, the more we suffer. The more solidly we see things, the narrower our world becomes, and our whole life situation becomes stuck and unworkable. Thus the practical value of emptiness is not really on the object's side (the fact that everything lacks real existence), but it is on the subject's side. This refers to the experience of letting go of clinging to real things and thus not being under their sway anymore, instead relaxing into that experience's true nature of infinite openness, freedom, and wakefulness.

When we talk about emptiness, the big question is what is this "emptiness"? It is probably easier to say what it is not, and that is usually exactly what the texts do. They never say emptiness is this or that. That would be like shooting ourself in the foot because emptiness means that we cannot pinpoint anything, including emptiness. Therefore, if we describe it as "something," we are back to square one. So let's look at what emptiness is *not*.

First, emptiness is not some kind of spiritual atom bomb that destroys everything that we know (though it may seem that way sometimes because it crashes the hard drive of our ego-mind with all its stored belief systems). Second, emptiness does not mean that phenomena are not empty as long as we do not analyze them and then they become empty when we analyze them. Emptiness is not some kind of quality that is introduced through analysis. For example, it does not mean that if we do not analyze this table, it is absolutely real, and once we have analyzed it, either through quantum physics or Madhyamaka reasoning, it becomes empty. In other words, emptiness is not something that first does not exist and then becomes existent later. Third, we do not meditate on phenomena that are actually nonempty as being empty, thus making up some conceptually fabricated emptiness, which would be a more or less sophisticated type of brainwashing. Obviously that would not really work anyway. If things were in fact really existent, we would just impute some concept of emptiness onto them that would not change a thing. For example, no matter how much and for how long we may apply the notion of "whiteness" to coal, that does not do anything to change its blackness. Fourth, it is not the case that phenomena are nonempty as long as the wisdom of the noble ones has not arisen and then they become empty. In other words, it is not that once we are on the path of seeing everything becomes empty, while before it is not. Fifth, emptiness does not mean that something existed before and then it becomes nonexistent later, such as a candle flame dying out. It does not mean that things first are there and then they disappear when we realize them to be empty. In other words, emptiness does not mean extinction. Sixth, emptiness does not refer to utter nonexistence, such as the horns of a rabbit or the hairs of a turtle. Seventh, in itself emptiness is not something holy, precious, some kind of universal law, or some sort of divine principle to be venerated. However, the realization of emptiness is something very precious and worthwhile because it eliminates confusion and suffering. Eighth, emptiness is not something that exists in some other dimension apart from phenomena. It is not yet another thing or concept that floats above everything. That is, if we talk about the two realities, it does not mean that seeming reality is one thing over here and ultimate reality is another thing over there, because then we could never speak about the inseparability of the two realities. Also, if we, for example, talk about the emptiness of a glass, if we destroy the glass, where is the emptiness of the glass? It is not there anymore, which means that emptiness is always the emptiness *of something*. The only exception of that is the emptiness of emptiness, but that is a different case altogether. Likewise, when we talk about the union of appearance and emptiness, this means that, without appearance, there is no emptiness either. In other words, emptiness is simply the true nature of what appears and therefore cannot be something apart or outside of what appears. Finally, emptiness does not refer to one thing being empty of another, such as a vase being empty of water, our pocket being empty of money, or a horse being empty of being a cow. In fact, the Buddha said that this is the worst type of misunderstanding emptiness.

What is the problem with all those mistaken kinds of emptiness? They are either some kind of limited emptiness, mentally contrived emptinesses, or emptiness in the sense of extinction. None of them refers to emptiness as the utter groundlessness of our being, which is the only chance for liberation. In more technical terms, true emptiness means that everything is empty of a nature of its own. In other words, emptiness does not mean that a glass is empty of something else, such as water or being a table, but that the glass is empty of being a glass. If we look for the "glassness" of the glass, so to speak, we cannot find it. We do not even need Buddhism for that; quantum physicists tell us the same thing—there is no glass to be found anywhere. What we see as a glass is just something that our eye consciousness makes up; we could say it is some kind of condensed energy that our eye consciousness perceives as a certain color and shape. In addition, our perception of a glass is very conditional because other sentient beings perceive this "glass" in a completely different manner. For example, the eyes of flies or fish show a very different picture of what we perceive, and some animals cannot even perceive certain colors.

Therefore, even on a relative level, it is highly questionable whether there really is a glass out there, something solid and real that we can actually identify. The more we look into it the more it becomes clear that there really is not anything out there. Since we cannot step out of our mind, we cannot even check to see if there is something out there or not. We would have to leave our own way of perceiving the world behind and compare it with some other hypothetical world of perception, which begs the question, "Who would perceive that world?" We only have our one mind and cannot compare it with somebody else's mind. Even if we could, that would still be subjective on our part because we cannot make such a comparison but from the perspective of our own mind. So we would need some kind of referee with an "objective" perception of how the world out there really is, but obviously there is no such thing. Even if there were, there would be no way for any one of us to ascertain this "objective perception" because we are confined to our own subjective perceptions. We would have to take on the mind of that other person, which, of course, does not work.

Therefore, if we analyze all those things that seem to be so real, we find that they are not just less real than they seem—they are completely unreal. Also, it is not just a matter of different people seeing the same thing in different ways, such as different people seeing an actually existing external glass or a person in different ways. In fact, everybody has their own movie going on in their mind, which is their own little private reality. There is no one thing that is just seen in different ways—there is no thing in the first place. From the mahāyāna Buddhist point of view, whatever appears just appears in our mind and the reason why humans, for example, generally seem to perceive the same things is that they have a certain amount of similar habitual tendencies for similar perceptions. But if we look into the details, nobody ever has the exact same perception as any other being. Even if we think we see the same table in front of us, in fact we all see something different. Some see the front side of the table, some its back side, some its left, some its right, some its upper side, and some its underside. In fact, nobody can ever see the entire table at one time. What we all do, however, is to conceptually supplement our different and partial visual perceptions with the parts of the table that we do not see and then call this compound of perceptions and concepts a "table," which makes us think that we all really perceived the same thing. If we just went with the data that our immediate sense perceptions provide, we would all the time only deal with snippets of what we consider a table and so on, which would make communicating very difficult.

Also, based on our previous experiences, we are constantly anticipating a lot of things with regard to what we see. Merely seeing a delicious piece of pizza makes us anticipate its taste and smell and our mouth starts to water. Even if we do not touch and lift a table, we still expect it to have a certain texture and a certain weight. When we see a glass, we know that it is fragile and if somebody throws a glass at us, our reaction is either to catch it or duck. All those many superimpositions onto our plain visual perception of a certain color and shape immediately become a part of what we call "a glass" or "a table," and that part is huge compared to what we actually see. Our visual perception does not tell us any of this, but our conceptual mind adds all these details by projecting previous experiences onto new objects. If we ask our eyes what they see, the answer is very simple—some color and shape. But if we ask our conceptual mind what we saw, such as a glass, the answer is not simple at all and instead we get all this blah blah blah. By contrast, small children deal with objects without any, or with very little, anticipation, which is why they usually tip them over, smash them on the floor, or do all kinds of, from our perspective, weird things with them. If we throw a ball at a small child, there is no reaction whatsoever until that ball actually hits the child (I am not suggesting doing that . . .). The child just sees some color and shape moving, but has no concepts about that color and shape, such as that it is a ball and that it will hurt once it makes contact.

That process of ongoing conceptual superimposition also makes it so wonderfully easy to project anything onto what we perceive as "others." We do not usually project that much on things such as a glass (except when we own a very expensive one and then it breaks), but we can see how much we project onto persons. Different people project all kinds of things, but none of these projections have much or anything to do with that person. If there really were some person out there, at least somebody's perception should be right, but our own perception of that person keeps changing and the person also keeps changing. Thus, there is not really much to hold on to here, which is the basic message of emptiness—things being empty of a nature of their own and being unfindable, yet at the same time still appearing. That is why the *Heart Sūtra* says later, "Form is emptiness; emptiness also is form." It does not just say emptiness is emptiness, but that emptiness and form are not separable—form is nothing different from emptiness and emptiness is not different from form. The two are always in union.

Strictly speaking, it is even trickier because there are no "two" in the first place. Ultimately speaking, relative appearances are not really there in the first place since they are just like illusions. Thus the union of appearance and emptiness is like the appearance of a mirage, for example, something that looks like water appearing on a road on a hot sunny day. There is no water on the road, but it seems to appear by virtue of a number of conditions, such as hot air right above the road, sunlight, and us looking at a certain angle, which leads to the clear sky being reflected within that hot air on the road in front of us.

Also, ordinary beings can only perceive and cling to dualistic appearances, while missing out on their emptiness. Noble beings in their meditative equipoise just see emptiness, in which there are no dualistic appearances at all. At least as ordinary beings, we cannot switch back and forth between appearance and emptiness. Unfortunately, we cannot take a comparative perspective, saying, "Now I see relative reality and now I see ultimate reality." On the other hand, once we perceive ultimate reality, we do not see dualistic relative reality anymore, at least not in our own perception.

So why is it so important to understand what emptiness is and what it is not? The only reason why the Buddha taught emptiness was in order to liberate sentient beings from suffering and enable them to attain omniscient buddhahood. The Buddha did not introduce emptiness as some kind of smart theory, linguistic game, sophisticated philosophical or metaphysical concept, or some sort of metalanguage. His sole concern was to teach it as something that helps beings to become free and experience lasting happiness. Therefore, emptiness is a pedagogical tool, but, in itself, it is not of intrinsic value or existence. It is a means to point out to people how things really are because they suffer due to their confusion of not seeing how things really are. When emptiness is understood correctly as taught by the Buddha, emptiness serves as the single suitable foundation of the path to liberation and omniscience and as the remedy for all afflictive and cognitive obscurations, while the above types of mistaken emptiness do not fulfill these liberating functions. That is the reason why it is important to understand exactly what the Buddha meant by emptiness and not to just pick up yet another theory or clever idea that we can add to our already overflowing bin of mental garbage.

Especially in the midst of all the technicalities, reasonings, and concepts that we find in presentations of emptiness, we need to remember this essential point: emptiness is a tool to free our mind. That is its fundamental purpose. When we talk about emptiness, it is easy to forget this and wonder, "What are we doing here?" Then it is good to come back to the basic purpose of the Buddhist path, which is liberation from saṃsāra and its suffering. In other words, emptiness has a very practical purpose. It is not just something to be understood and then we move on, wherever we are in saṃsāra. As the experiences of those arhats with heart attacks show, emptiness is really meant to shatter saṃsāra not just in an intellectual sense but in a very tangible experiential sense, which means connecting to the fundamental groundlessness of our experience.

Of course, groundlessness sounds scary, but it is just one side of the coin of liberation. Emptiness is groundless in terms of saṃsāra or our ordinary ego-based existence, but at the ground or the bottom of that saṃsāric groundlessness there is a more fundamental ground, which is called buddha nature. Unless we dare to look at the groundlessness of our illusory existence, it is very hard to penetrate to the actual and reliable ground of our existence. The tricky thing is that a big part of that reliable ground is groundlessness. As long as we do not face that groundlessness and integrate it into our mind, there will not be any solid ground whatsoever. The only reliable ground is to live with and within groundlessness, not in a state of constant panic or dread, but fully accepting that this is the way things are. Then we can simply join the dance of fleeting appearances and not feel the need to resist this dance by trying to freeze its constantly changing appearances. This is not at all scary. It is a tremendous relief and pleasure to cast off our long-term burden of desperately trying to hold things together. It only sounds scary because we always try to hold on to something and are afraid of letting go. But as soon as we are not holding on to anything, this is ultimate freedom because we can go anywhere and we can do anything without getting stuck or blocked.

For example, if we sit in a plane before attempting our first jump with a parachute, we do not really want to jump and we hold on to our familiar ground, which at this point is the plane. But once we let go and actually take the leap, it is total freedom. We can fly around in space wherever we want and in any way we want. While we are flying, we do not have any thought that we need to hold on to something, that we have to pull the brake, or that we need to go back into the plane. There is just the experience of unlimited freedom, spaciousness, and joy. It really depends on our own mental outlook. Two seconds before we jumped we were scared and tried to hold on to anything we could get our hands on, but once we are in the air our hesitations are gone and the power of the experience of flying takes over. Likewise, whether groundlessness sounds scary or like freedom depends on our mind and whether we still want to hold on to something or not.

It is like Janice Joplin sang, "Freedom's just another word for nothing left to lose." That is exactly the point of the teachings on emptiness. As long as we feel there is something to lose, no matter what it is, we are still bound and hooked. Having nothing left to lose might sound depressing, but once we are actually there, it is totally liberating. There is nothing that can confine us at all and whatever we experience in that spaciousness is like a gift that can only be received when we are completely open. We do not have to run after things to get something nor do we have to avoid anything because whatever comes up is just fine. In the movie *Kung Fu Panda*, the master, who is an old turtle, speaks about the past, future, and present, saying:

> The past is history, the future is a mystery, but today is a gift—that's why they call it "the present."

If we are in the present moment, whatever happens is a gift. We can see that we do not even have to study the *Heart Sūtra*; it is all out there already.

The place where emptiness hits its own ground—or rather its own groundlessness—is called "the emptiness of emptiness." When we deal with emptiness, there is still the danger or the tendency to solidify emptiness itself. Though it is meant as the final antidote for clinging or solidifying, our mind still tries to solidify even the very lack of solidity since it is such an old habit of ours. This is why the Buddha taught the emptiness of emptiness, meaning that we need to let go of whatever understanding of emptiness we may have too since it is not the real thing. We need to let go of any sense of insight, realization, or wisdom, any sense of "I got it," because that still involves duality, solidification, and reference points. Since emptiness means that there is nothing to solidify and nothing to hold on to, it defeats the purpose if we make emptiness into some kind of principle, universal law, or higher truth because then we are still holding on to something.

It might be slightly better but it could also be a lot worse if we hold on to emptiness, because that usually means that we miss out on the compassion part. We might just think, "Oh, yes, everything is empty, nothing really matters." However, that is not an understanding of emptiness at all; it just means being stuck in nonexistence and nihilism. The teachings on emptiness always say very clearly that emptiness is not nonexistence or sheer nothingness. Nonexistence is just another headache, it is just another thing that we make up. Nonexistence still depends on existence and we cannot even conceive of nonexistence if we have not previously thought about existence. In other words, for any negation there must be something that we can negate in the first place. We cannot negate nothing whatsoever to start with; we must have something and then we can negate it and say, "I ended up with nothing." But that "nothing" only works in dependence on the "something" that was there before. Emptiness points out that both existence and nonexistence are just superimpositions that, moreover, depend on each other and that we have to go beyond existence and nonexistence. However, to go beyond existence and nonexistence does not mean that phenomena are both existent and nonexistent, nor does it mean that they are neither existent nor nonexistent. None of these theoretical options gets us out of the box of dualistic mind. Existence is one extreme and nonexistence is another one, so if we put them together, how does that make things any better? It is even worse to blend two mutually exclusive possibilities and think that this is more sophisticated (though it is extremely popular to do so). If we say "neither existence nor nonexistence," it maybe sounds smart but "neither" is still based on the previous two mistaken options of existence and nonexistence.

Of course, we could go on and on like that, but we are screwed every time because we are still depending on what we came up with before, just trying to wiggle our way out of the last option that did not work. That is why emptiness means to completely step out of this cycle of dualistic mind and all its ramifications, dropping anything that we have ever conceived of. Naturally this is very hard because creating concepts about everything is what we do all the time. It is the essence of dualistic mind to set up black-and-white categories and then rearrange them and combine them in all kinds of ways. Emptiness simply means, "Just stop that, drop it now." However, this is difficult because it does not tell us what we should do instead. Since we are so used to always *doing* something, it is completely against the grain to not do anything at all. *Undoing* cannot be done; it is not another kind of *doing*, not even the opposite of doing. We are basically left with nothing. No previous experience or strategy is of help here; we need to let go of everything we know and then see what happens.

The Fourfold Profound Emptiness

The remainder of what Avalokiteśvara says in the *Heart Sūtra* represents his more detailed answer to Śāriputra's question and is also a commentary on the meaning of "seeing the five skandhas to be empty of nature." The first four phrases of this longer answer are often regarded as the heart of the *Heart Sūtra*:

> Form is emptiness; emptiness also is form. Emptiness is no other than form; form is no other than emptiness.

This slightly more detailed answer is also known as "the fourfold emptiness" or "the fourfold profundity" (a bit further down there is also "the eightfold profundity"). This is the key statement in the *Heart Sūtra* as well as in the prajñāpāramitā sūtras in general. It sounds as if form and emptiness are exactly the same, but that is to be taken with a grain of salt. What this passage talks about is the unity of the two realities, with "form" representing seeming or relative reality and "emptiness," ultimate reality. Why is form empty? Because it is empty of a nature of its own. Why is emptiness form? Because it is nothing but emptiness that appears as form. If we look for any form that exists independently apart from emptiness, we do not find any, and if we look for any emptiness apart from form, we do not find that either. For example, as long as a flower is there, the emptiness of the flower is also there. But if there is no flower, there is no emptiness of the flower either. Fundamentally, the emptiness of all phenomena is the same, but relatively speaking there are different emptinesses in relation to different relative objects. The larger prajñāpāramitā sūtras list twenty emptinesses in dependence on different bearers of emptiness or different objects that are empty. Thus we can speak of the emptiness of a flower, the emptiness of a glass, and so on.

Of course all of that only makes sense from a relative point of view—we refer to whatever appears and then we talk about the true nature of whatever appears. However, if nothing appears at all, we cannot talk about the true nature of that. So we have to have something, however flimsy it might be, that we take as our object or reference point and only then can we talk about the true nature of that object. We are not talking about the true nature of nothing whatsoever, but we are talking about the true nature of "something," because "something" is what we experience in the world. We never have an experience of nothing whatsoever nor do we deal with nothing; we always experience and deal with *something.*

Thus the phrase "Form is empty" means that form does not have any nature of its own. In other words, form is empty of being form. "Emptiness also is form" means that what appears as form is inseparable from emptiness. In fact, emptiness is the very reason that anything can appear at all because emptiness is the fundamental space, nonsolidity, and openness in which appearance, movement, functionality, and change are possible. If things were solidly and independently existent, nothing could ever appear newly or change. If the world arose at all, it would always be the same as in the first moment it came into existence. If things were independently existent on their own, they could not function or interact at all. Once things interact, such as functioning as causes and their results, they become dependent on other things. That is why Nāgārjuna said that it is precisely because of emptiness that things appear and function. It is precisely because phenomena are not solid and independent that they can change; otherwise everything is completely static and frozen.

The sūtra continues by saying, "Emptiness is no other than form; form is no other than emptiness." Why are form and emptiness not different? Emptiness does not exist apart from form, nor does form exist apart from emptiness. We cannot find any emptiness of a glass that is separate from the glass, nor can we extract the emptiness of the glass and put it next to it. When we talk about the emptiness of a glass, it is bound to the appearance of the glass; the one cannot appear or exist without the other. On the other hand, form and emptiness are not the same either. The emptiness of the glass is not the glass itself, otherwise we would see emptiness when we see the glass. Emptiness is the nature of form and form is that which bears emptiness as its nature. We cannot say that the nature of something is that something. Otherwise it does not make any sense to speak of two things—that something and its nature. Thus form and emptiness are mutually exclusive in the sense of there not being any common locus for them. That is, there is nothing about which we can say that it is both form and emptiness. However, in the sense of it being impossible that the one exists without the other, we can say that form and emptiness are of the same nature.

Are Form and Emptiness Two Things?

Ultimately, however, there is only emptiness, or ultimate reality, so the question of whether form and emptiness are the same or different is moot because there are no two things to compare in the first place. We cannot ask whether a single finger is the same or different. Still, from the perspective of conventional or seeming reality, we can speak about form and emptiness as being two, but even then they cannot be said to be the same or different.

According to the *Saṃdhinirmocanasūtra*, there are four flaws that would follow if the two realities—or appearance and emptiness—were one and the same. (1) Just as ordinary beings perceive the phenomena of seeming reality, they would see ultimate reality at the same time. For example, we would see emptiness just by seeing a flower. Emptiness would be something that is accessible through our ordinary sense perceptions because it is the same as the forms and so on that our senses perceive. Therefore, while still ordinary beings, we would be liberated without effort and achieve nirvāṇa or buddhahood. That would also mean that the entire Buddhist path is useless. (2) The defining characteristics of seeming reality and ultimate reality would be mutually inclusive. From this it would follow that, for example, the emptiness of a desirable object is also an object of desire and thus a cause for suffering rather than its remedy. (3) Emptiness, or ultimate reality, has no diversity, whereas there is a lot of diversity in the phenomenal world of seeming reality. But if the phenomenal world of form were the same as emptiness, there either would be diversity in emptiness or no diversity in phenomena. (4) Yogic practitioners would not have to seek for an ultimate reality beyond conditioned phenomena as they appear to the senses or as they are conceived by the thinking mind.

If the two realities were different, this would also entail four flaws. (1) Those who see ultimate reality would not be liberated from saṃsāra and achieve nirvāṇa or buddhahood. For the experience of seeming reality would not be affected in the slightest by seeing ultimate reality because they are completely unrelated. For example, to see a flower does not eliminate seeing a table. Or it would be like taking antibiotics to cure high blood pressure. (2) Ultimate reality would not be the true nature of the conditioned phenomena of seeming reality since they are two completely separate things, just as a vase is not the true nature of a piece of cloth. (3) The mere emptiness or the sheer lack of nature of conditioned phenomena would not be their ultimate character since ultimate reality and seeming reality are completely unrelated. For example, the lack of nature or the emptiness of a glass, that is, the fact that it does not really exist on its own, would not be the true nature of the glass because the two realities are different. When we talk about the lack of the nature of a glass, that lack is still related to the glass, otherwise we could not call it the nature of the glass. If it were something completely different, we could not say it is its nature, just as we cannot say that a flower is the nature of a glass. (4) Afflicted phenomena and purified phenomena— that is, mental states of basic ignorance with their delusive appearances and the nonconceptual wisdom that realizes emptiness—could simultaneously exist within the mind streams of noble beings, such as buddhas, since the realization of emptiness would not have eliminated ignorance, just as a table does not eliminate a chair, whereas poison can be eliminated by its antidote.

In addition, the statement that form is emptiness and emptiness is form also serves to avoid the extremes of superimposition and denial—superimposing real existence onto seeming reality and denying appearances altogether. Some people might think that what appears to our senses and our conceptual mind is all there is; they think the only reality is whatever there is in front of their eyes. They superimpose too much existence onto the fleeting illusory appearances of seeming reality, putting all their stock in mere appearance. On the other hand, some people might say, "There is nothing at all because it is all empty." That means to deny even mere illusory appearances and wrongly equate emptiness with utter nothingness.

"Form is emptiness; emptiness also is form" also counteracts one-sided clinging to either appearing forms or emptiness alone, or entertaining some form of eternalism or nihilism, respectively. Therefore, it shows the middle way between these extremes. In terms of the view, the famous middle way means not to fall into clinging to just appearance or clinging to just emptiness, but to see that appearance and emptiness are inseparable. In that way, we are not getting stuck on either one. We do not make things more solid than they are and we do not deny that there are fleeting and ever-changing illusory appearances. This is called "the union of the two realities." Again, this is not just some logical or philosophical exercise, but it refers to the experience of how our minds react to things that we take to be more real than they actually are. For example, if we take a movie for real, we get totally carried away by the story line. We might even cry tears or yell, "Kill him!" This comes from superimposing too much onto mere appearances because all there is are moving light dots on a screen. The actual story of the movie is really happening nowhere but in our mind. That means we watch two movies—the outer movie on the screen, for which we have to pay, and the inner movie in our mind, which is free and usually much more entertaining. If there were no people with minds to enact and enjoy the actual movie in itself, anything that happened on the screen would be completely pointless.

This shows how our minds deal with appearances that we take too seriously. We ascribe more reality to appearances than they actually have, and then we get caught up in them and invest in them emotionally, financially, and in many other ways. Basically it is a setup because our point of departure for the whole thing is already mistaken, so no matter what we do afterwards, it will not really lead to any proper outcome in terms of how things actually are. For example, if we fall in love with one of the characters in a movie and try to pursue that person, it will never work out. On the other hand, if we just say, "Nothing is happening at all," we are in denial that in terms of relative reality certain things actually *do* happen and we are subject to them. Obviously we cannot just pretend that nothing is happening when we are kicked out of our apartment, do not pay our bills and taxes, keep driving when the lights are red, and so on. Of course, we can forget about all that once we have realized emptiness as Avalokiteśvara has, but for as long as we experience relative causes and their effects, we cannot ignore that type of reality and need to work with it in appropriate ways.

"Form is emptiness; emptiness also is form" can also be understood as indicating meditative equipoise without appearance and the periods between formal meditation sessions that entail appearance, respectively. It also refers to the eventual union of being and not being in meditative equipoise in a buddha. What actually happens is that emptiness and appearance appear together at the same time, but the question is whether we actually perceive just the one or the other or both. On the level of mere appearance, which is our ordinary experience, what appears to our visual consciousness is nothing but shape and color, and emptiness is not something that appears to our sense consciousnesses. When bodhisattvas on the bhūmis enter meditative equipoise and directly perceive emptiness, ordinary appearances disappear within that equipoise. For beginners as well as such bodhisattvas, the perceptions of appearances and emptiness are mutually exclusive—either we perceive the appearance or we perceive the true nature of the appearance. However, when bodhisattvas rise from their meditation, appearances appear again, but not as solidly as for ordinary beings because there is a certain degree of carrying over of their experience and realization within meditation into their experiences when they do not meditate and engage in other activities.

In conclusion, "form is emptiness" refers to the emptiness of the phenomenal world, counteracting the extreme of believing in the absolutely real existence of fleeting phenomena such as form. "Emptiness is also form" indicates that nothing but emptiness arises as dependent origination, thus putting an end to the extreme of believing that nothing exists at all. "Emptiness is no other than form" presents the union of appearance and emptiness or the inseparability of emptiness and dependent origination, thus rejecting the extreme of being both existent and nonexistent (or eliminating the two extremes of nihilism and existential absolutism at once). "Form is no other than emptiness" signifies that appearance and emptiness are not incompatible, but necessarily supplement each other in perfect harmony, thus negating the extreme of being neither existent nor nonexistent. In this way all possibilities of how we mistakenly conceive of phenomena as existent, nonexistent, both, or neither are transcended, which constitutes the total freedom from all expressions, thoughts, and reference points.

The Middle Way without a Middle

As discussed before, the realization of emptiness makes everything much lighter. Therefore, bodhisattvas do not perceive a glass in the exact same way that we do, nor do they cling to its real existence anymore. It is more like a lucid dream. It is not that that nothing at all appears, but bodhisattvas are increasingly able to sustain their realization of emptiness within everything that appears, no matter how intense it may be. What appears becomes lighter and lighter, and finally there is no difference between being in meditation and not being in meditation because the realization in meditation carries over fully into any other activities and experiences.

This is what the middle way means in terms of view and practice. Strictly speaking, in terms of the view it does not even mean a middle between two things. For example, when we talk about existence and nonexistence there is no real middle between them, such as something that is half existent and half nonexistent. If we think that there is some middle, we just have found another thing to latch on to. In terms of conduct, there is definitely a middle way because there is still something to do. What the Buddha originally taught as the middle way was the middle way between asceticism and hedonism, the middle way between overindulgence in sense pleasures and torturing ourselves. However, in terms of the view, we cannot really talk about a middle way or even a middle because that would mean to identify something. Any time that we identify something, it is not emptiness or ultimate reality because we still have some reference point and something to stand on. This is not groundlessness or the freedom from reference points.

Therefore, some Tibetan masters interpret the Tibetan word *uma* for middle or Madhyamaka as meaning "not even a middle." In other words, the middle way in terms of the view is that there is not even a middle, let alone any extremes or opposite poles. For example, if we hold up our two index fingers in front of us, we can identify the middle of the space between the two finger tips, but if we take away those two fingers, where is that middle? Therefore, if the reference points that define a middle are gone, we cannot find or talk about a middle anymore either. If we insist and keep gazing at the point in empty space that we identified as the middle before, we are just stubbornly holding on to some conditional point of reference that is not there anymore once the conditions have changed. It is like insisting that New York is in the east when we are somewhere in Europe just because it is in the east when we are in Seattle. From a Madhyamaka point of view, anything that we might identify as a middle is just another extreme or just another reference point, so "middle" is just a shorthand for the fact that there are no reference points at all, be they extremes, a middle, or anything else.

That is also the reason why the prajñāpāramitā sūtras and other texts often say, "To not see anything is the supreme seeing." This does not literally mean to see nothing at all in the same ways that blind persons or people who are asleep do not see anything. As the Buddha said:

> Beings usually speak of "seeing the sky."
> Examine this point of how you see the sky!
> The Buddha taught that the seeing of phenomena is just like
>   this.

What are we really seeing when we say, "I see the sky"? We may say, "It is this blue expanse." So we take it as something blue up above us, but we know that there is no such blue thing up there. We are looking into a void that appears to us on the earth as blue due to certain conditions. Once we look at the earth from outer space, there is no blue sky at all. In this way the sky is an example of something that appears in a certain way but what we are actually looking at is something completely different. Therefore, when we think about what it means to "see the sky," it means to see appearance and emptiness in union. When we see the sky, what we are actually looking at is space, but we cannot see space because space is the absence of anything. If we see something, we do not call it space but we call it "something." If there is something, there is no space in that place, the space is literally taken up. In the case of the sky, space mostly appears blue, but sometimes it also appears red, orange, yellow, or purple (at dusk or dawn), white or grey (with clouds), or even green (with northern lights). Nevertheless, it is still the same space. Likewise, when we look at a table, though its appearance is based on more heavy-duty habitual tendencies of reifying, if we ask quantum physicists, they also say that when we look a table, we are basically looking at space.

Question: If the table in front of you is empty, how can it still support a glass?

KB: We can look at the same thing from the ultimate and the relative point of view, but it gets very confusing if we mix those two perspectives. We cannot put a really existing glass on an empty table. If we look at the table and the glass from the ultimate point of view, both are equally empty and there is nothing that serves as support or supported. But if we look at them from the relative point of view, an illusory table can very well support an illusory glass in an illusory manner, just as a table in a movie is seen to support a glass. However, we cannot use a reason that pertains to ultimate reality to disprove relative reality and vice versa. We cannot say, "Things are not empty because I can see and touch this glass." Nor can we say, "There is no glass at all because all phenomena are empty." That would be to confuse the two levels of reality, which is obviously not what is meant by the union of the two realities. A main reason the Buddha taught these two realities was in order to be clear about on which level of reality we are talking about phenomena, that is, whether we speak from the perspective of what ordinary beings perceive as their reality or from the perspective of what those who see how things actually are perceive as ultimate reality. In fact, the majority of misconceptions about the Buddhist view stem from not understanding the distinction between seeming and ultimate reality.

A frequently used example for the relationship between dualistic appearance and emptiness is what people with cataracts see. These people may see all kinds of weird things that actually do not exist, such as little black dots when looking at a white surface, or two moons in the sky. Once the cataracts are removed, they see the white surface without dots or the sky with just one moon. Likewise, from the viewpoint of ultimate reality, form or the obscurations in general are as illusory as those dots or the two moons. When we talk about the union of appearance and emptiness, for ordinary beings it is like the dots in space. It is not really that they do not see the space around the dots, but that they totally zero in on the dots. In our ordinary perception, if we look somewhere, our focus is not on the space around things, but it is on the things within that space where we always get stuck. We do not really pay attention to the space but we always deal with the appearances in space. Likewise, it is not that emptiness does not appear for ordinary beings, but we miss it because we are totally carried away by the appearances within emptiness.

As long as we are under the influence of the disease of ignorance and dualism, we are not aware that appearances do not really exist and we try to deal with them as if they were real. In the case of cataracts, we may think that there are black dots on the white sink and try to wipe them off, which obviously does not work. So, first some physician has to tell us that these dots are just something caused by cataracts in our eyes and that they are not really out there. However, even if we understand that the dots are not really out there, they still appear. Therefore, the next step is to schedule an operation to remove the cataracts, after which we will not see any dots again. This does not mean that the operation removes all visual objects or our entire eye, but that we regain clear eyesight. Likewise, the process of effectively removing the disease of ignorance with its many symptoms of dualistic appearances starts with studying and reflecting on the Buddha's teaching. However, just understanding emptiness in all its ramifications does not make dualistic appearances vanish because they are based on very strong habitual tendencies. It is only through meditation or thorough familiarization with emptiness that the disease of ignorance is removed, after which dualistic appearances will not arise again. In other words, our conceptual understanding of emptiness needs to sink in and become an intrinsic part of the fabric of our mind. For us as ordinary beings it is completely natural to take all things to be solid and real by virtue of our having deeply ingrained habitual tendencies, but we can equally familiarize ourselves with emptiness so that it becomes equally natural to see the lack of real existence in everything.

Question: People seem to have different ideas about what space is. Can you clarify the notion of space a bit more and whether that space is empty too?

KB: In Buddhism space is defined as the absence of anything. However, the whole notion of space is basically just a concept because we cannot really perceive an absence with our senses. We can see a glass, but we cannot actually see the absence of a glass. We always say, "Yeah, I see the space," but we do not see the actual space, we just do not see a thing within that space. In fact, we always see something, but we can never see "nothing." For example, we may look at two chairs and say, "I see the space between these chairs," but what we are actually seeing between these two chairs is the floor or the wall. We usually treat space as an actual thing and even think that it performs functions, such as providing space. However, in Buddhism, space as the absence of anything is not a thing nor can it perform any functions. Space does not actively provide space, such as someone exiting a crowded room so that we can enter. Nor does it really open the door and say, "Welcome phenomena, come in and move around, be my guest." In any case, whether we take space as a concept or as a mere absence, it is as empty as anything else, that is, not existing with any intrinsic nature of its own. Neither the concept of space exists on its own nor the sheer absence of anything exists on its own. In other words, if we analyze where that space is or what it is exactly, it is even more obvious than with a table that we cannot find it. With the table we can at least conventionally say how long, wide, and high it is and which color it has, but with space we cannot determine any of this.

It seems there are always a lot of problems around the notion of space, which is somehow quite telling. In Buddhism space is understood as the very absence of obstruction, within which things that entail obstruction can move around and interact. If the entire space would be full of things, nothing could ever happen, similar to a room that is crammed full of things up to the ceiling. In such a room there is no space to enter, let alone to move around in. It seems that our minds are sometimes like a room full of things in which it is very hard for anything to move—everything seems to be static and fixed. On top of that, if we try to pull out one thing, the rest might just avalanche us. So either we just leave it as it is or we need to be careful with starting to move things around .

Question: Does the example of ice and water relate to the two realities being neither the same nor different but still having some relationship? *KB*: Yes, very much so. If we have a chunk of ice, we cannot say that its being ice and its being water are the same or different. When water has turned into ice, it is not water because it does not look the same and it does not perform the same functions as water does. For example, we cannot drink it or do our laundry with it. But at the same time we cannot say that this water and ice are two entirely different things because the nature of ice is water. Also, we cannot really pull out the water from the ice and put it next to the ice. Either there is an appearance of water or there is an appearance of ice; we cannot have the two as distinct phenomena at the same time. Likewise, we cannot pull out emptiness from a table and put it next to the table, but in terms of how emptiness and the table appear, we cannot say that they are exactly the same either.

Question: As for the terms "relative reality" and "ultimate reality," "relative reality" seems to refer to appearance and "ultimate reality," to emptiness. But sometimes "relative reality" is explained as the way in which ordinary beings perceive things and "ultimate reality" as the way in which bodhisattvas and buddhas perceive things. So there seem to be two ways of understanding these terms.

KB: The first explanation is from the perspective of the objects, while the latter is from the perspective of the subjects that perceive those objects. The Eighth Karmapa said that when we speak of ultimate reality, it does not exist anywhere else but in the minds of those who perceive it. Ultimate reality is not an object that exists somewhere out there and then we stumble upon it. There is no ultimate reality or relative reality independent of the perceiver. Rather, whether we experience ultimate or relative reality is a question of whether we have transformed our entire mental outlook. This complete transformation of how we see ourselves and the world is then called "ultimate reality" because a change of the perceiving subject entails a change of the object it perceives. For as long as there is ignorance in the mind stream there is delusion producing deluded forms of objects, just as with those black dots that someone with cataracts sees. From the point of view of somebody who does not have cataracts, the perception of black dots is mistaken because those dots do not appear to someone without that disease. In order to regain unmistaken perception we neither can nor have to remove the dots, but we need to work on the eye as the perceiver. Likewise, we do not need to remove appearances but work with how we perceive and cling to them. As Tilopa said to Nāropa:

> It is not the appearances that bind you, but your clinging to these appearances. Therefore, let go of your clinging, Nāropa!

Also, when we talk about seeing pure realms and stuff like that, it is not that we get an upgrade of appearances or that we check out of one set of appearances and enter a different superior set. What changes is our perception.

An example to illustrate that the difference between relative and ultimate reality lies in the eye of the beholder, so to speak, can be found in books like *Magic Eye* that have been around for a few years. These books contain two-dimensional pictures, and if one looks in the right way, one can suddenly see a different three-dimensional picture instead of the two-dimensional one. Obviously, the two-dimensional picture has not changed physically, but we see something that was not there before simply because our way of looking has changed. From that example we can see how dramatically our outlook can change even on a simple and conventional level. So if we extrapolate that further, we might get an idea of what is possible in terms of perceiving ourselves and the world in a completely different way in terms of ultimate reality. To see the two-dimensional pictures is like seeing mere appearances without any emptiness, whereas seeing the three-dimensional ones illustrates seeing the union of appearance and emptiness.

It is also interesting to consider the manner in which we need to look at those two-dimensional pictures in order to see the three-dimensional ones. The more we focus on the existing two-dimensional picture and try to see something else the less it actually works. Instead, when we relax our eyes and basically look through the two-dimensional foreground without focusing on it at all, the three-dimensional background suddenly pops up. Similarly, the prajñāpāramitā sūtras always talk about "not focusing" and "not observing" phenomena and that this is the highest form of seeing, that is, seeing ultimate reality. So maybe those books such as Magic Eye are the modern "Prajñāpāramitā Sūtras for Dummies."

Question: The experience of ultimate reality, even if it is fleeting, happens spontaneously or instantly, so does compassion arise equally naturally along with that experience? In other words, does the experience of great compassion or care for all beings spring from the realization of emptiness?

KB: A realization of emptiness without compassion is impossible. However, it is not that once we realize emptiness we suddenly jump from no compassion to limitless compassion for all sentient beings, as this realization definitely depends on having previously cultivated compassion. Just meditating on and realizing the ultimate—emptiness—is unfortunately not enough; the path to buddhahood involves many other practices on the level of relative reality in order to cultivate and enhance compassion and to put it into action. Compassion is often compared to the moistening quality of water in that it moistens our mind stream, thus making it supple, flexible, and fertile. If we lack compassion, our mind is like some very old dry piece of leather. It is very rigid and almost lifeless, no matter how much insight into emptiness we might have. If we have an overemphasis on the prajñā of realizing emptiness, our mind can become like that stiff leather or like a sharp sword, which cuts very well but has no heart. That is why we speak of "emptiness with a heart of compassion." Once emptiness is fully realized, there is also full compassion precisely because there is no sense of self anymore. This means that all the energy of our mind that used to be sucked into that black hole of ego-clinging is set free. So what does it do? It just goes outward to others. All the energy of our mind that is set free is radiating outward, reaching out to others, because that is what the mind naturally does if it is not confined by clinging to a self and the real existence of phenomena.

We could say that our clinging to a self is like boiling water in a steam pot with a tight lid. The water in this pot cannot go anywhere, it just turns into very hot steam swirling around rapidly. The whole situation is claustrophobic and painful in there. But once we open the pot, the steam spreads in all directions, cools down, and moistens everything. There is no more pressure, confinement, or pain; instead it swirls around naturally and more playfully, enjoying its freedom. In that way we could say that our mind behaves like water. We can heat it up and put it under a lot of pressure, but once we take away its confinement of ego-clinging and the heat of our mental afflictions, just like water it cools down and naturally spreads everywhere. This is how emptiness and compassion go together. To realize emptiness means to realize that there is no confinement and that our mind can move freely. If we let it move freely, what it does is compassionate reaching out to others, seeing that there are no boundaries between ourselves and others. It is like reaching out to the other pressure cookers and helping them open their lids.

Question: In order to directly perceive ultimate reality is there anything to be transformed other than our conceptual mind?

KB: Our conceptual mind is the most superficial level of all the layers of our mind that need to be transformed. In Buddhism we speak about six or eight different types of consciousness. The more superficial consciousnesses are the five sense consciousnesses and the conceptual consciousness, while the more subtle ones consist of the "afflicted mind" and the "ālaya-consciousness." The latter is the most fundamental level of our dualistic mind and represents the sum total of our ignorance about how things really are, which consists of the latent tendencies for everything that appears as objects and the consciousnesses that perceive them. The other seven consciousnesses and their objects emerge from and settle back down into the ālaya-consciousness, just as waves rise from and sink back down into an ocean. The afflicted mind is the part of our mind that confuses the ālaya-consciousness for our self and clings to it in that way, thus tainting all our perceptions, thoughts, and emotions from the perspective of our ego. In addition to these eight primary consciousness, there are also a lot of mental factors, such as feeling, discrimination, anger, desire, ignorance, prajñā, and so on. On the path we work with all of these and they all become transformed or change their state. Many texts explain in detail how the eight consciousnesses emerge as their true nature, which are the five kinds of buddha wisdom that we discussed above. In brief, the ālaya-consciousness becomes mirrorlike wisdom; the afflicted mind, the wisdom of equality; the conceptual mind, discriminating wisdom; and the sense consciousnesses, all-accomplishing wisdom. The dharmadhātu wisdom is the fundamental expanse of mind within which all this happens.

Though conceptual mind is the most superficial level of consciousness, it is the one that we usually deal with the most. Therefore, many Buddhist teachings recommend that we work with our thoughts in a skillful way instead of trying to get rid of them, which does not work anyway. This is also why it says in the Mahāmudrā tradition that "thoughts are the dharmakāya," which is saying the same thing as "form is emptiness." It does not literally mean that our thoughts, just as they appear, *are* the dharmakāya, because then we are done here. It means that the nature of our thoughts is the dharmakāya. In the example of ice and water, we cannot really say that ice *is* water, but the nature of ice is water. This means that the ice can change into water, not through transforming miraculously, but because it is already in its nature. We do not have to manipulate the ice to become water—in its essence it is already water. Likewise, thoughts or anything that appears in our mind bears mind's true nature in it, so it is a matter of letting that nature come forth.

Question: When we work on penetrating the boundary between self and other, is that prajñā or compassion?

KB: It is both. From a mahāyāna Buddhist point of view we cannot really dissolve the boundary between self and other through compassion or emptiness alone. Both have to go together. If we try to do this through compassion alone, there is still a certain clinging to ourselves and to real existence, which prevents us from fully dissolving all the borders. If we try it with emptiness alone, we have the problem of the approach being too cold and clinical, with not enough heart in it. It is not just a technical process, like tearing down a wall between us and others, because there is an affective emotional quality within this process. If that is lacking, it does not work. We could say that it is not enough just to tear down the walls between us and others, but we also need to reach out and talk to these others. If we just tear down the walls and stay on our side of the wall while they stay on their side, then we are still disregarding those other people and there is no connection, like close neighbors who see each other every day but never talk and do not know anything about each other. So emptiness or prajñā is very good for tearing down the walls, but in order to actually relate to others we need compassion or the outgoing energy of our mind. Prajñā is not what does that because prajñā only cuts through and removes the obstacles to genuinely reaching out. Therefore, we need both, prajñā and compassion are a package deal.

At the same time, it is important to see that prajñā and compassion enhance each other. For example, if we have an overwhelming feeling of compassion, the borders between us and others naturally dissolve temporarily. In fact, we completely forget about ourselves and there is no sense of separation but only boundless empathy. At the same time, if we have some sense of the unreality or illusionlike quality of phenomena, the borderlines between us and others become much more transparent too and we can see better who these others actually are and that they suffer just as we do.

When we hear all these things about emptiness we sometimes may wonder where the heart is in all that. If we just talk about it from an intellectual point of view, it often sounds very analytical and dry. But if we think about what compassion is, it really means to have no self, as illustrated by the English word "selflessness." If we have no ego and no self-concerns, what does our mind do? It does not mean that we just go to sleep or become some vegetable, but it means that there is a lot of energy that is freed up to naturally extend ourselves to others. I think we all have experiences of that.

All Elements of Our Body and Mind Are Like Space

This ends our discussion on the fourfold profundity of "Form is emptiness; emptiness also is form. Emptiness is no other than form; form is no other than emptiness." However, this fourfold profundity not only applies to form and emptiness, but also to the remaining four skandhas of feelings, discriminations, formations, and consciousness. Therefore, the *Heart Sūtra* continues:

> In the same way, feeling, discrimination, formation, and consciousness are emptiness.

When understood properly and fully, the brief explanation "form is emptiness and emptiness is form" already covers all phenomena. However, for those who need more detailed explanations, the same principle can be applied to the other skandhas, such as the one of feelings (which is probably by far the largest skandha of Western people, whereas it is quite small in the East). Discrimination mainly refers to the conceptual level of making distinctions between things through discriminating their characteristics, such as big and small or good and bad. The skandha of formations includes all the mental factors that are not contained in the second, third, and fifth skandhas, such as those that always accompany every state of mind, the primary and secondary afflictions, and the virtuous mental factors. The skandha of consciousness consists of the above-mentioned six or eight consciousnesses. All these skandhas are the same in that they are inseparable from emptiness.

The Buddha provides us with the five skandhas as a checklist of phenomena so that we do not miss out on any of them. We may agree that form is emptiness and emptiness is form, but what about feelings, which seem to be much more vivid and real. Or we may think that our consciousness is not empty. Each skandha in turn has many subdivisions, so they are like a detailed checklist for our entire psychophysical existence in terms of both body and mind. In the foundational Buddhist approach the skandhas are mainly used for checking whether there is actually a truly existing self anywhere within our body or mind. In order to not just do that on a coarse level, but on a subtle level, we can go through all those subdivisions of the five skandhas and we will not miss any constituent of our existence.

This process is a little bit like when we are looking for a key in our house. Our house has a lot of rooms, which are like the five skandhas, so we run through all the rooms and we look. If we do not find the key, we run through those rooms again and also look in all our closets, all our drawers, under the bed, and so on, which are like the subdivisions of the five skandhas. Once we have checked every little spot in our house several times and we have not found our key, we can be sure it is not in the house. Likewise, we search for our self in our five skandhas and when we do not find it anywhere, we need to conclude that there is no such self altogether because our self or ego cannot be anywhere else than in our body or our mind, such as in our car. Though, I guess, some people's self might actually be in their car . . . The point of the five skandhas is to give us an exhaustive list of places to look for our self. Unlike in the key example, where the key could still be in our car or somewhere else outside our house, the skandhas include all possible places for our self. In terms of our experience and not just as a philosophical concept (such as an *ātman*), there is probably no one who thinks that their self is actually somewhere outside of their own body and mind.

So this is the foundational Buddhist approach in terms of there being no personal self in the skandhas, but the *Heart Sūtra* goes even further. It not only says that there is no personal self in those skandhas, but that the skandhas themselves do not really exist either. If we dismantle our entire house piece by piece and we still do not find our key, we can be absolutely sure that it has not been in the house. But here we are not just looking for the key of the self that does not exist in the house of the skandhas, we are destroying this house altogether, which is the most thorough way of searching for our existence.

The Eightfold Profundity

To make that really clear, the *Heart Sūtra* continues with what is called "the eightfold profundity":

Thus, Śāriputra, all phenomena are emptiness, without characteristics, without arising, without ceasing, without stain, not without stain, without decrease, and without increase.

This means that all phenomena are not only empty of any intrinsic nature or real existence, but also lack the remaining seven features.

No Exceptions in Emptiness

As for "all phenomena are emptiness," the five skandhas include all conditioned saṃsāric phenomena, which are also called "afflicted phenomena." However, there are even more dharmas, or phenomena, that is, unconditioned phenomena (such as space) and purified phenomena. The prajñāpāramitā sūtras say that, no matter which phenomenon we take, it is empty. These sūtras list 108 sets of phenomena, fifty-three afflicted phenomena and fifty-five purified phenomena. Ostensibly, the prajñāpāramitā sūtras try to get rid of the seventy-five dharmas of the abhidharma, but then they bring in even more phenomena. However, they do not introduce all these phenomena in order to say that they are better than the ones of the abhidharma, but in order to show that those phenomena do not work either. Also, after having demolished all the abhidharmic phenomena, the prajñāpāramitā sūtras even bring in all the phenomena of the path of the mahāyāna and say, "Forget about those too."

Strictly speaking, the sūtras do not recommend forgetting about those phenomena right away. They ask us first to become familiar with them, see what they mean, and use them in our practice, but also to see what they actually are, which is empty of any nature of their own. This includes not only all saṃsāric phenomena, but all phenomena of the mahāyāna path and its fruition, starting with bodhicitta, the bodhisattva bhūmis, all the meditations, experiences, and realizations on the path, as well as the omniscience of a buddha. It makes sense that even the wisdom of a buddha is no exception to being empty because once emptiness is fully realized, there is nothing to pinpoint, so how could buddha wisdom be something that could be pinpointed? Also, if this wisdom were really existent, this would mean that something static would have the infinite outlook on the dynamics of the infinity of dependent origination, which cannot possibly be. In other words, the ultimate perceiver and the ultimate object have to be in tune—the only way to perceive the freedom from all reference points is not to have or entertain any reference points. This means that a buddha's mind has a panoramic scope and openness, without being stuck on anything. As long as we hold on to anything in our perceiving mind, this means that we do not have a vast outlook but are glued to some illusory reference point.

Still we may wonder, "What is the point of introducing all kinds of things, such as the paths and bhūmis, that we haven't ever even thought about before and then saying that they do not really exist anyway? Why not just leave things as they are?" That is actually exactly what the Buddha would like to do the most, but unfortunately it does not work as a path to freedom. It is like in that Zen saying: "First the mountains are mountains. Then the mountains are not mountains. Finally the mountains are mountains." This sounds weird, but that is how it is. First we unquestioningly think that mountains are mountains, which means that we have a lot of conceptual overlay. Then we dismantle all of that overlay, which means that there are no mountains as we used to see them anymore. Finally we just see what is actually there, which is the appearance of what we call a mountain without any conceptual overlay. Even if we try to be simple, it is very hard to jump to that third stage unless we have dismantled all our conceptual overlays and imputations.

The abhidharma attempts to describe its version of ultimate reality as being a multiplicity, mapping out the world and saying that everything in it is real. The mahāyāna presents the entire phenomenal variety that appears on a conventional level, but then it says, "Ultimately, none of these phenomena really exist." The prajñāpāramitā sūtras only give us all these long lists in order to make sure that we do not miss out on any phenomenon, thinking that this one must actually exist while all the others do not. As Wittgenstein said, "Philosophy should be entirely simple." Well, the outcome is entirely simple but the process unfortunately is not because we have to work with our complicated mind. If we have a very simple mind, simple methods will do, but most people do not have a simple mind. We can check which category we ourselves belong to by counting how many times we ask "why." If we ask "why" a lot, we are definitely not in the category of simple minds. As long as we keep asking "why" we are still looking for more answers and are not ready to let go.

In a contemporary commentary on the *Heart Sūtra* from the point of view of quantum physics it is said that when the sūtras talk about all phenomena, they are very much like the point instances in quantum mechanics or like the wave-particle duality. That means how those phenomena appear and how they behave depends on how we focus on them. In quantum physics all those phenomena are described as being very elusive and not even existing in a strictly material way. Basically, all those phenomena are just portrayed as fleeting moments of appearance, and the clearer that becomes, the more and more obvious it becomes that they are empty of any solid or lasting existence. Quantum physics says that those wave particles, subatomic particles, or whatever we want to call them are not something that we can really find, because they are defined as a complex of relationships, which is a very dynamic and immaterial idea of what such a "particle" is. Usually when we think about a particle or an object, we think it is something static because this is what our low-tech perception freezes it into. In actual fact, however, everything that we perceive is a dynamic process. Not only is our perceiving mind dynamic in that it changes from moment to moment, but the objects are too. From the emptiness point of view, or more positively phrased, on the side of dependent origination, phenomena cannot be defined by themselves, rather we can only talk about them as complexes of mutual relationships with other phenomena, which in themselves are complexes of relationships with other complexes of relationships. Both quantum physics and Buddhism say that phenomena are like a constantly changing criss-cross of an infinite number of waves on an ocean or fleeting fluctuations in an immeasurable field of free-floating energy.

Of course, we do not perceive phenomena in that way. For example, when we watch a movie, we do not really see all the separate pictures on the film, which are much more than we can perceive, but our perception blends them together. There are thirty-two pictures per second, but we take them to be one object. Maybe we should watch movies by looking at the film rather than the screen.

The Looks of the Daughter of a Barren Woman

As for the *Heart Sūtra* saying that all phenomena are "without characteristics," usually Buddhism speaks about general and specific characteristics. For example, a general characteristic of the sound of a bell is that it is impermanent. The characteristic of being impermanent is common to all conditioned phenomena such as sounds, but we can also identify the specific characteristics of the sound of a specific bell at a specific time, such as its duration, its pitch, its rhythm, and so on, which distinguish it not only from any other sound but from any other phenomenon. In the abhidharma both general and specific characteristics are said to be really existent. But here, both are said to be empty in that they do not exist in any intrinsic manner.

When we understand emptiness, it is implied that there are no characteristics. If all phenomena are empty of a nature of their own, they are also empty of characteristics. If we still get stuck on the characteristics, it means we have not really understood the emptiness of phenomena. For example, if a flower does not really exist in the first place, it is moot to talk about any of its characteristics—it is like discussing the looks of the daughter of a barren woman. Still, the *Heart Sūtra* speaks about the lack of any characteristics because though the lack of characteristics is logically implied by emptiness, this does not necessarily mean that that lack is fully realized. Even if we understand that a flower as such is empty, we could still get stuck on some of its impressive apparent features, such as its vivid colors or its wonderful smell, and then have second thoughts about its lack of real existence. Sometimes we solidify the characteristics of a thing even more than the actual thing. For example, we may have a very nice car which was very expensive. We treasure it a lot and we get completely stuck on all its wonderful features. It does not even matter anymore whether it is a car or a cow or anything else because it is *our* car, so precious, so cool, and so impressive when shown to others. This is also a reason why the *Heart Sūtra* says that all phenomena are "without characteristics." We can use this as a reminder when we get carried away by the characteristics of something, be they good or bad. This also means that there are no characteristics of affliction and purity, that is, there are no characteristics in terms of some phenomena binding us in saṃsāra and others liberating us from it. There are no characteristics or differences between saṃsāra and nirvāṇa, they are all just imputations onto empty appearances.

All Phenomena Are Unborn and Unceasing

The next two features of "the eightfold profundity" are

without arising, without ceasing.

We could also say, "There is no birth of anything and thus no cessation." This is what the Madhyamaka texts talk about all the time—"no arising" is one of their big themes. When Madhyamaka texts investigate all phenomena's emptiness through reasoning, they use two main approaches. One is to directly analyze the nature of an object and the other one is to analyze its characteristics. These two approaches correspond to the *Heart Sūtra's* above two phrases that "all phenomena are emptiness" and "without characteristics," respectively. Either approach is good enough, but the one works better for some people and the other one works better for others. Also, as mentioned above, they complement each other and make sure that we understand the full scope of emptiness. When we analyze the nature of a flower, for example, the classical reasoning is to examine whether the flower is really one or many and to see that it is neither. If we cannot find anything that is the "flowerness" of the flower, which would be the one thing that is its essence or constitutes it, then what appears as a flower is not a multiplicity either because any multiplicity has to be made up of many "ones." Conventionally speaking or in terms of mere appearances, of course, we can say that a flower is "many" because it consists of many parts. However, that is not the point here because when we analyze each part of the flower, we find even smaller parts, which can be split up further in an infinite progression. This reasoning investigates whether the flower is something that truly and independently exists as one single thing, something that we can identify, pinpoint, isolate, extract, or nail down as its final indivisible essence, similar to modern physicists looking for "the final smallest particle" as the ultimate unchanging true nature of phenomena. However, if we cannot even find a truly existing "one," we cannot find any truly existing "many" either.

If we really understand this, it is enough for understanding the emptiness of a flower and we do not have to worry about its characteristics. But if we are not satisfied with the reasoning of the lack of one and many, we can also take the second approach and double-check by examining the characteristics of a flower, such as whether it really arises at some point or not. Conventionally speaking or in terms of mere appearances, of course, flower seeds grow into sprouts, which eventually blossom, but when we look into this growth process, we cannot find any real arising anywhere. Usually, in Madhyamaka, arising is analyzed through cause and result. That is, we analyze whether there is any real relationship between cause and result at all. Generally, in order for something to arise the cause has to precede its result. Otherwise we do not really speak about causality. There seem to be certain exceptions in modern physics in terms of the result preceding the cause, but in terms of our experience, which is what we are talking about here, causes have to come before their results. If we think that a flower really arises, there must be some relationship between its cause and the result. Madhyamaka reasoning takes this to a momentary level, which means that in the moment in which a given cause exists, its result is not there yet. In the next moment, when the result is there, the cause does not exist anymore. This is the principle of causality. Cause and result cannot exist simultaneously, otherwise we would not consider them as cause and result in the first place. If they existed simultaneously, why would we need that cause, since the result is there already? The fact that two things exist simultaneously shows that they are not a cause and its result because the result cannot exist together with its cause, just as a flower does not coexist with its seed.

If we look at this temporal sequence of cause and result and if we see that, at any given moment, there is always either only the cause or only its result, then how could the cause ever do anything to the result? How could it produce the result because they never even meet or have contact? What kind of interaction could there be? For example, if there is a room with two doors and one person enters the one door exactly at the same moment another person exits through the other door, they do not even see or meet each other, let alone have any interaction. Therefore, it is said that there is no true arising. Conventionally speaking it seems to work, but if we analyze how results could arise from their causes, the answer is that they do not really arise from them.

The classical Madhyamaka reasoning that investigates arising based on cause and result is called "the vajra sliver reasoning." If things really arise, they must arise either from themselves, from something other, from both, or from neither (that is, without any cause). Most people think that things arise from something else, following the usual notion of causality in which the cause is different from the result. However, as we just saw, in that case cause and result never meet or interact. If things were to arise from themselves, they would arise all the time because as long as the thing in question is there, it must function as its own cause and thus constantly reproduce itself, otherwise it is not a productive cause. So we would end up with the whole universe being filled with self-produced things. And if a thing arises from itself, the cause is useless or pointless because that thing exists already. If we combine both possibilities, saying that things arise from both themselves and others, it may sound like a smart solution. Conventionally speaking, a clay pot may be said to arise from itself in that it is made from a rather amorphous lump of clay, while it also arises from others because it is made by a potter's hands, a potter's wheel, water, and so on. However, if, as we just saw, each of the possibilities of arising from itself and arising from others does not hold up under investigation, how would adding up two wrong possibilities make it any better? It just gets doubly wrong.

Finally, some people say that things simply arise spontaneously without any causes or by chance. This is a very convenient concept that we always use if we cannot or do not want to explain something, saying, "Oh, well, it just happened." However, that does not work either because if things arise without any cause, the whole universe would be completely random and anything could happen at any time. When we wake up in the morning, we would have no idea what will happen in the next moment— our bed or our house might suddenly disappear and some jungle with wild animals could arise instead. That things arise without any cause also contradicts our daily experience because any goal-oriented activity that we engage in is based on accumulating certain causes in order to gain certain results. Otherwise, activities such as farming or preparing a meal would be completely pointless because we would never know what happens next and any cause that we set would not have any effect.

So then what? If things do not arise from any of these four possibilities (themselves, others, both, or neither), where does that leave us? It leaves us literally nowhere. This approach is typical for the prajñāpāramitā sūtras and Madhyamaka. They consider all the possible ways that something could happen or exist and then check them off one after the other as not working. Through these four possibilities of arising we have exhaustively identified every possible manner of arising. We might try to come up with a fifth or sixth possibility, whatever that would be, but that does not make it any better, because all conceivable possibilities are included in those four. Once we have seen that none of those four works, we can become depressed or irritated, or we can look at our mind, which is the intent here. Through eliminating all four possibilities of real arising, we have exhausted our conceptual dualistic mind that clings to arising; we beat it with its own weapons, so to speak. We always think, "If it is not A, then it must be B, and if it is not B, it must be A." We keep jumping back and forth between mutually exclusive possibilities. If neither works, we may think, "Maybe it is both A and B" or "Maybe it is neither A nor B." As long as we do that, we are still in the ballpark of dualistic mind. So the only solution here is to step out of this ballpark altogether and let go of jumping around from one dualistic reference point to the next.

In that way, the process of doing these kinds of investigations as to whether phenomena are one or many or do arise is literally a process of exhausting our conceptual and dualistic mind. This is also exactly what koans do. Though Madhyamaka reasonings are much more wordy and complicated, their desired effect on our mind is exactly the same as that of koans, which means getting us to a place where we can take a leap, leaping out of our cage of dualistic mind. However, since we don't usually ever do that, it often takes a while for us to be ready to leap. When we work with koans, it takes a while before we realize that there is no one or right answer anyway. In the Madhyamaka reasonings too, it is not about the answer, they are not trying to tell us how things *really* are. They are trying to tell us, "That's not it, that's not it, and that's not it." At the point of having exhausted all conceptual possibilities, we need to look inside, look back at our mind and see what it is doing in this situation. What is the one who did that analysis experiencing right now? What is the one who stripped away all those reference points feeling now? Our mind is still there and experiencing. If we conclude those reasonings, we do not drop dead nor do we just dissolve into empty space. There is still the experience of the one who did the analysis and stripped away all kinds of mistaken ideas.

This is why the Mahāmudrā and Dzogchen traditions speak of "naked mind." We take off all its conceptual costumes, one after the other. If we do not look at our naked mind at the end of that process of undressing, it is pointless. We are just left with a big heap of useless stripped off clothes, but we never get to see what has been inside them. It just becomes mental gymnastics or, in the worst case, we end up in some sort of nihilism. This is where the idea of freedom comes in, when we go through such reasonings or recite the *Heart Sūtra*. Once our conceptual mind is exhausted, there is the gap, there is the chance for something different to happen. Of course neither Madhyamaka nor the *Heart Sūtra* tells us what that might be, and for good reason, because we would immediately grasp at that "something" and thus fall back to square one. We cannot be naked when we take off all our regular clothes and then put on this really fancy new dress. In other words, we cannot contrive being uncontrived.

"Without arising" also means that there is no arising from ignorance. The only way that phenomena can seem to arise on the level of conventional reality is because of our ignorance about how things actually are. Once we are convinced that there is no real arising, there is naturally no real ceasing either, that is the easy part. What does not come from anywhere does not go anywhere. Or what never arose at any point in time cannot cease at any point in time. In other words, there is no arising of something that did not exist before and there is no ceasing of something that did exist. Usually when we talk about arising we think that something did not exist and then it somehow suddenly becomes existent. After it has existed for a while, it ceases, thus becoming nonexistent. However, even on a conventional level, if we accept causality, it is never the case that something comes out of nothing or that something becomes nothing, disappearing completely. For example, a tree comes from a seed and that seed comes from another tree, and so on. Even if the tree rots away, its substance does not vanish altogether, but it becomes earth and then other plants grow out of this earth. A tree consists of all kinds of different substances or chemical molecules and when it decays it just means that the tree's macroscopic form disappears, whereas its molecules do not disappear, but are simply rearranged in different ways, such as first becoming earth and then becoming part of a new plant. It is sort of the same soup all the time, just being stirred in different ways.

"Without ceasing" also means that there is no real cessation of ignorance since ignorance does not really arise in the first place. Thus, on the path we do not really have to destroy or deport some really existing ignorance because it is basically just a misperception, just like mistaking a hose with a zigzag pattern for a snake. Once we take a good look at that "snake," we see that it is not a snake and thus our ignorance that it is not a snake dissolves naturally. When we realize that there never was any snake in the first place, we can see that our perception of a "snake" never really existed either.

Phenomena and Emptiness Are neither Pure nor Impure

The next pair among "the eightfold profundity" is

without stain, not without stain.

No matter how confused or ordinary phenomena may seem, since they are not different from emptiness, there are no truly existent stains that need to be removed, just as there is no truly existent ignorance to be eliminated. Phenomena are not really stained, nor are they the stains, nor is emptiness stained by them. "Stain" can also be interpreted as the activity of our mind apprehending and clinging to objects. Or we can say that buddha nature is not stained within sentient beings. Buddha nature is always unchanging, no matter whether it is the buddha nature of an ordinary being or the buddha nature of a buddha. It does not become any better or worse. According to the Eighth Karmapa, it is not that sentient beings *have* stains, but they *are* the stains. So we can also say that buddha nature is not stained *by* sentient beings.

Thus, since there are no real stains, there is no stainlessness either because "having no stains" depends on "having had stains." Even from the perspective of the elimination of stains there is no stainlessness because, ultimately speaking, all phenomena—the stains—are emptiness, luminosity, and fundamental purity, in which there never is any stain whatsoever. It is like the impossibility of a snow flake in the raging fires of hell or of darkness in the middle of the sun. Likewise, mind's luminous nature is too overwhelming for any stains, there is simply no room for them and they have no chance of existing there. This is also the meaning of the nature of thoughts being dharmakāya, which means to realize that there never have been any stains in the first place. To realize this is liberation, but when it is not realized it is called "saṃsāra," "ignorance," "thoughts," "obscurations," and so on. Finally, another meaning of "neither with nor without stains" is that the skandhas are neither different from nor the same as emptiness.

Nothing to Be Added and Nothing to Be Removed

The sūtra concludes "the eightfold profundity" with

without decrease, and without increase.

One way to explain "decrease and increase" is that they stand for the extremes of nonexistence and existence—things decrease and then they are gone, or things arise and then increase. Emptiness is completely free from any decrease or increase of anything. Decrease and increase can only happen with conditioned and impermanent phenomena, while emptiness does not work that way. Decrease and increase can also refer to sentient beings versus buddhas in the sense that we might think that there is some decrease of buddha nature or the nature of mind in sentient beings, meaning that it is not as good as the nature of the mind of a buddha. We often think, "I can see that the nature of the mind of a buddha is really awesome, but the nature of *my* mind?" No decrease or increase can also mean that buddha nature exists in every sentient being, even in tiny animals such as mosquitos, without any deterioration, while it does not increase in quality in buddhas. We might think, "Is the buddha nature in a mosquito really as good or as big as my own or the one in a buddha?" Obviously when we talk about buddha nature or emptiness, we are not talking about something that has any size, dimension, or limitation.

Without decrease and increase can also refer to faults and qualities, respectively. On the path there is no real increase of good qualities of the mind nor is there any real decrease of flaws. For what we perceive as flaws also is something that does not really exist in the first place. Flaws never arose, came into being, or increased, like an increasing heap of garbage in a movie, and therefore they cannot decrease either. On the other hand, the qualities of the nature of the mind are there all the time, so they can neither decrease nor increase. Whatever appears as a decrease of flaws and an increase in qualities on the path is nothing but the gradual uncovering and seeing of the natural qualities of mind's nature. After all that has been said so far, it should be clear, however, that those qualities are not something solidly existing that we can pinpoint either. The prajñāpāramitā sūtras emphasize again and again that if we think we have found something on the path, such as relinquishments, realizations, or attainments, we have not found any of these things, but something else, which is yet another version of our basic clinging to really existing phenomena.

The fundamental quality of the nature of the mind is precisely that it is infinite, spacious, and without any reference points. That is the freedom aspect, this tremendous space. But it depends on how we look at that space, whether we freak out about its groundlessness or whether we see it as an unlimited potential. For example, some people are claustrophobic, others are agoraphobic, and some enjoy vast spaciousness, but their widely divergent responses are all reactions to the experience of space. Those who want to read in more detail about how buddha nature does not increase on the path or in buddhas, and how it does not decrease in sentient beings, can study the *Uttaratantraśāstra* by Maitreya, which contains many instructions and examples relating to that.

The Three Doors to Liberation

The constituents of "the eightfold profundity"—phenomena being empty, having no characteristics, no birth, no cessation, no stains, no stainlessness, no decrease, and no increase—are included in "the three doors to liberation," which are emptiness, signlessness, and wishlessness. The prajñāpāramitā sūtras speak about these three all the time. The door to liberation that is emptiness refers to the true nature of phenomena. Signlessness means that all causes are without any signs or characteristics. Wishlessness refers to all results not being something to be wished or hoped for. Since everything is empty and we cannot pinpoint anything that would characterize any causes either, there is really nothing to hope for. The bodhisattva path is a completely hopeless situation, not in a depressing way, but in a manner of not being attached to any particular outcome or achievement. Therefore, bodhisattvas are totally open to and ready for any development in a given situation or person and they cannot be disappointed either. This is actually one of the main characteristics of bodhisattvas—to have no expectations, and as the counterpart of that, no fear either (which is actually mentioned later in the *Heart Sūtra*). From the perspective of the perceiving subject or nonconceptual wisdom, the door to liberation that is emptiness is represented by the samādhi of observing the two kinds of identitylessness (the lack of a personal identity or self and the lack of any identity or intrinsic nature of phenomena). The door of signlessness corresponds to the samādhi of observing the skandhas—the bases of these two types of identitylessness—as being erroneous. The door of wishlessness is the samādhi of observing nirvāṇa as the cessation of the skandhas.

So how are the eight profundities included in the three doors to liberation? The first two—that phenomena are empty and without any characteristics in general—refer to the door to liberation that is emptiness. The next four—no arising, no ceasing, no stains, and no stainlessness—refer to the door of signlessness or the lack of more specific characteristics of phenomena. The last two—no decrease and no increase—refer to wishlessness. That is, if we really understand that there is no decrease and no increase, there is nothing to expect and nothing to fear.

The commentary on the *Heart Sūtra* by the Tibetan master Padma Karpo says that the door to liberation of emptiness is explained in the sūtra through everything from the beginning up through "Thus, Śāriputra, all phenomena are emptiness." The door of signlessness is discussed by the following passage: "without characteristics . . . no mental consciousness dhātu." The next section up through "no nonattainment" explains the door of wishlessness.

The sūtra continues:

> Therefore, Śāriputra, in emptiness there is no form, no feeling, no discrimination, no formation, no consciousness . . .

As you remember, Avalokiteśvara's short answer started with "Form is emptiness; emptiness also is form" and then he said that the same goes for feeling, discrimination, formation, and consciousness. This was followed by "the eight profundities," which apply to each one of the five skandhas. Now Avalokiteśvara basically sums it up and says that all five skandhas do not exist in emptiness, just as there are no clouds in a bright clear sky. Or, in contrast to the above statement of "form is emptiness; emptiness also is form," which describes the general view of the inseparability of form and emptiness or the two realities, this passage can be understood as specifically referring to the nonconceptual meditative equipoise of bodhisattvas on the bhūmis, during which the five skandhas do not appear. Forms, feelings, smells, tastes, and tangible objects have characteristics, while emptiness consists of the very lack of characteristics.

More Ways of Slicing the Cake of Illusory Phenomena

The next lines present two further sets of phenomena, which are basically two more ways to slice the big cake of phenomena:

no eye, no ear, no nose, no tongue, no body, no mind; no form, no sound, no smell, no taste, no tangible object, no phenomenon; no eye dhātu up to no mind dhātu, no dhātu of phenomena, no mental consciousness dhātu . . .

The passage "no eye . . . no phenomenon" lists the twelve āyatanas and the passage "no eye dhātu . . . no mental consciousness dhātu" refers to the twelve dhātus. Unlike the five skandhas, which include only all conditioned phenomena, the āyatanas and dhātus represent two slightly different ways to classify all conditioned and unconditioned phenomena. In particular, it is the āyatana of dharmas, or phenomena (which is identical to the dhātu of phenomena and consists of the objects of the mental consciousness), that includes both conditioned and unconditioned phenomena. Among conditioned phenomena, the āyatana of phenomena includes everything in the skandhas of feeling, discrimination, and formation. According to the *Abhidharmakośa*, this āyatana also includes three unconditioned phenomena: (1) space (the nonobstructive absence of any conditioned phenomena), (2) analytical cessation, and (3) nonanalytical cessation. Analytical cessation refers to becoming free from the clinging to a self and the ensuing afflictions and suffering through the prajñā of realizing the lack of a personal self. Nonanalytical cessation refers to something simply not existing or happening in a certain place due to the absence of specific causes and conditions (for example, horns not growing on the head of a horse). Other sources refer to four types of unconditioned phenomena, listing the fourth one as suchness.

The *Abhidharmasamuccaya* lists eight unconditioned phenomena: (1) space, (2) analytical cessation, (3) nonanalytical cessation, (4)–(6) the three suchnesses of virtuous, nonvirtuous, and neutral phenomena, (7) the meditative absorption without discrimination, and (8) the meditative absorption of cessation. The meditative absorption without discrimination is the highest type of meditation within the fourth meditative level of the form realm (the fourth dhyāna). When practiced for a long time, this type of meditative absorption leads to rebirth on the highest level of the gods of the form realm. This kind of absorption is characterized by the temporary cessation of all consciousnesses and mental factors with an unstable continuum (the five sense consciousnesses and the mental consciousness plus their accompanying mental factors). However, mistaken appearances will occur again when one leaves this meditative absorption because the latent tendencies for the arising of these consciousnesses still exist. The meditative absorption of cessation (a. k. a. "the meditative absorption in which discrimination and feeling cease") represents the cessation of all consciousnesses with an unstable continuum as well as some with a stable continuum (the first seven consciousnesses and their mental factors, i.e., omitting the ālaya-consciousness). On the Buddhist path one employs this state as the culminating meditative absorption in the process of "ninefold progressive abiding." This consists of various ways to train in entering into and rising from the four dhyānas of the form realm as well as the four absorptions of the formless realm, which represent increasingly subtle and clear forms of *śamatha* (calm abiding). Based on using such refined śamatha, one can cultivate the Buddhist *vipaśyanā* (superior insight) of realizing the lack of a self and phenomena.

Literally, "āyatana" means "support" or "abode." Thus, the twelve āyatanas act as the sources or gateways for consciousnesses and mental factors to arise. The āyatanas also enable the movement of consciousness in terms of subject and object. They consist of the six inner āyatanas (the six sense faculties) and the six outer āyatanas (their six objects from visual form up to the conceptual phenomena of the thinking mind).

In the lower Buddhist schools and conventionally in the mahāyāna, the first five sense faculties (eyes, ears, and so on) and their respective objects have the nature of matter. Unlike the five sense consciousnesses, the sixth one—the mental consciousness—does not rely on any physical sense faculty, but instead depends on the "mental sense faculty." In general, any given moment of consciousness cannot arise without a preceding moment of consciousness. What is called "the mental sense faculty" is simply the fact that the ceasing of a preceding moment of consciousness triggers a following moment of consciousness. This applies to all six consciousnesses, but it is specifically referred to as the "mental sense faculty" because it represents the most specific condition for the arising of the sixth consciousness, which lacks any physical sense faculty. Note that the immediately preceding moment of consciousness does not necessarily have to be of the same type as the following one. For example, it is not an immediately preceding moment of eye consciousness that gives rise to the first moment of the eye consciousness when waking up in the morning, but it is an immediately preceding moment of the ālaya-consciousness (or the mental consciousness). Also, a thought can arise based on the ceasing of any of the five sense consciousnesses or the mental consciousness. Therefore, the sixth inner āyatana of the "mental sense faculty" implicitly includes all six types of consciousness since any one of them can act as a preceding moment of consciousness. The corresponding objects of the mental consciousness are found in the sixth outer āyatana of phenomena.

As for the eighteen dhātus, "dhātu" literally means "element" or "constituent." The teachings describe a dhātu as a cause, seed, potential, or something that bears its own defining characteristics. In this way, the six outer dhātus (the five kinds of objects perceived by the five sense consciousnesses and the phenomena perceived by the mental consciousness) function as the causes, seeds, or potentials that are apprehended by the six consciousnesses. The six inner dhātus (the six sense faculties) function as the causes, seeds, or potentials that support the apprehension of those objects. The last six dhātus (the six consciousnesses) function as the causes, seeds, or potentials that act as the actual apprehenders of objects. Thus, when the sense faculties and their respective objects meet, a corresponding consciousness arises. In other words, the six outer dhātus represent the phenomena that have the characteristics of objects, the six dhātus of consciousness represent the phenomena that have the characteristics of the subjects which perceive these objects, and the six inner dhātus serve as the media that facilitate this apprehension of objects by their corresponding subjects.

In brief, the twelve inner and outer dhātus are identical to the twelve inner and outer āyatanas, and the twelfth āyatana (the mental sense faculty) implicitly includes the six dhātus of consciousness. Thus, the eighteen dhātus consist of the twelve āyatanas plus the six kinds of consciousness. In addition, the texts also describe the six dhātus that represent the elements or constituents of a person—earth, water, fire, wind, space, and consciousness.

You may wonder, "Are the five skandhas not enough? Why do we need to cut the cake of phenomena again through the twelve āyatanas and the eighteen dhātus?" In addition to the purpose of studying the five skandhas given above (which equally applies to the āyatanas and dhātus), the teachings also present the skandhas, āyatanas, and dhātus for the following three reasons. First, they enable practitioners to reverse the three types of ignorance. Second, they address people with high, medium, and lower faculties, respectively. Third, they engage those who prefer brief, medium, and detailed explanations, respectively.

As for the three types of ignorance, the skandhas are presented in order to remedy the ignorance of taking the mind to be a single unit. The majority of what is explained in the skandhas discusses the multiple types of consciousnesses and mental factors and thus counters this mistaken belief. The āyatanas remedy the ignorance of taking form or matter to be a single unit. Among the twelve āyatanas, eleven provide the various divisions of matter, thus challenging this type of ignorance. Lastly, the dhātus remedy the ignorance of taking both matter and mind to be a single unit because they outline the divisions of both matter and mind to an equal extent.

Furthermore, the skandhas, dhātus, and āyatanas are again like different fingers pointing to the moon. The skandhas are one set of fingers and the dhātus and āyatanas are others in order to point to the same things again, but from different angles. When we just read these lists in the *Heart Sūtra*, they seem to be repetitive because it says "no eye . . . no phenomena" and then further down it says, "no eye dhātu . . . no mental consciousness dhātu." Superficially, it all seems to be the same, but once we have actually studied the categories of the five skandhas, twelve āyatanas, and eighteen dhātus in a little bit more detail, we have a much more precise and vast sense of what phenomena actually are and what our reality consists of. We go more into the intricacies of what we experience every day, which means our ability to finely discriminate increases. If we read the sūtra with this background—and the original audience of the *Heart Sūtra* consisted of people who were well versed in the details of skandhas, dhātus, and āyatanas—its words become much more powerful because they strike every moment of our experience, saying about every moment of our experience, "Do not get stuck, do not get stuck." For example, when the sūtra speaks about the skandha of form, it does not really refer to form as one big lump of all forms, saying, "That big lump of form does not exist." Rather, it refers to every moment and every detail of every form that we may perceive at any time, indicating that these momentary appearances of form are ephemeral fleeting things with nothing to them. If we read the lists of phenomena in the sūtra in this way, it becomes very powerful because each word brings us back to the present moment.

Thus, we are not just talking about a concept of skandha or a general concept of form, but when we recite the sūtra we can take whatever perception we have at the time as our meditation object, right now in the present moment. In that way, the sūtra becomes a different experience every time we recite it because its words are directly related to the present moment of our experience, whatever it may be. That is why there is actually a point to all of those repetitions: their purpose is not just to exhaustively cover the entire scope of all phenomena, but to help us wake up on the spot—it is about nowness, the present moment of our experience. Otherwise, it would be sufficient to say, "All phenomena are emptiness, period, live with it." Of course, that is true and sufficient from a general point of view, but in terms of our experiencing many different moments of distinct and specific phenomena, it is too general. In order for the message of the *Heart Sūtra* to get through to us, we need to connect its words to the present moment of what is actually going on in our mind, otherwise it is just some superficial reading on a very conceptual level.

When we look at the larger prajñāpāramitā sūtras, they go into even finer detail in each one of these categories such as the skandhas, which means they are bringing us constantly back to our present experience. The freeze frame instant of our present mind is just like a bubble, and then there is another bubble and yet another bubble. The prajñāpāramitā sūtras constantly remind us of all those bubbles—they arise, but are evanescent appearances that do not really exist. Therefore, it is important to see the dynamic process quality of the whole enterprise of reciting the sūtra and not just take the words as mere lists of static things, which we check off one after the other like items on our shopping list. It is more like actually walking through the big shopping mall of all phenomena, looking at all the individual things that we wrote down on our shopping list, grabbing them from the shelf of dualistic solidification, and dropping them into our basket of appearance and emptiness being inseparable. All of this is a constantly changing process.

According to some commentaries on the *Heart Sūtra*, its passages on the nonexistence of the āyatanas and dhātus represent two sets of reasons for the immediately preceding passage of the five skandhas not existing in emptiness. In other words, if we are still somewhat stuck on the five skandhas and think, "Maybe there is something in them," we need to go deeper, which means to divide the five into the twelve āyatanas, and if that is not enough, we divide them into the eighteen dhātus. If that is still not enough, we divide them further until we arrive at our experience right now. The idea here is to go from a general conceptual level into being more and more specific. At the end of this line of investigation, the most specific thing that we can ever find is our experience in the present moment. This is as specific as it gets, which *is* the actual object of meditation, rather than all those more or less general categories. Naturally, the more familiar we are with those categories and all their subdivisions the easier it will be to come to that most specific moment of right now. If we have only a vague idea about the five skandhas, that is less helpful because we get stuck on the general concept. In brief, we could translate all the words in the lists of the prajñāpāramitā sūtras into "Look at your experience of the present moment, look at your experience of the present moment, look at your experience of the present moment . . ." instead of saying, "no eye, no ear, no nose . . ." and so on.

In particular, as decribed above, the inner and outer āyatanas are the gateways or doors for the arising of consciousness. According to the commentaries, they are also the gateways for the arising of characteristics. However, since the āyatanas, according to the *Heart Sūtra*, do not really exist, no eye consciousness arises from the meeting of visual form and the eye sense faculty and so on. The eighteen dhātus are the seeds or causes of characteristics, and since they do not really exist either, there are also no characteristics as the results of these causes.

Even Dependent Origination Is Emptiness

The sūtra continues with the twelve links of dependent origination:

> no ignorance, no termination of ignorance up to no aging and death and no termination of aging and death . . .

This refers to the twelve links from ignorance up through aging and death in their regular and their reverse orders. Up to this point, the sūtra has been dealing primarily with saṃsāric phenomena, such as the five skandhas. The twelve links in their regular order also represent saṃsāric phenomena in that they describe the process of how sentient beings arise, abide, and cease again and again based on fundamental ignorance. However, the sequence of the twelve links in their reverse order represents the manner in which the vicious circle of saṃsāra is broken. As mentioned above, to go through the twelve links from death all the way to ignorance is the main meditation of the pratyekabuddhas. Thus, this passage on the twelve links in the sūtra marks a turning point, switching from saṃsāric phenomena to the phenomena of the path that liberates from saṃsāra as well as the fruition of this path. In all Buddhist approaches of śrāvakas, pratyekabuddhas, and the mahāyāna, dependent origination is one of the most fundamental principles to describe both the process of saṃsāric confusion and suffering and the process of unraveling the web of such confusion. Thus, the twelve links of dependent origination are one of *the* hallmarks of the Buddhist teachings. However, the prajñāpāramitā sūtras not only trash saṃsāric phenomena such as the skandhas, but they also take on the hallowed principles of the Buddhist path itself. Therefore, the twelve links of dependent origination also get thrown out the window, in both their saṃsāric and nirvāṇic versions.

The essential point of the twelve links is that all phenomena of saṃsāra (skandhas, dhātus, and āyatanas) originate from ignorance as their starting point. From the perspective of relative reality, confusion comes from being ignorant about the relative nature of phenomena, that is, not seeing how dependent origination and karmic causes and results work (the first two of the four noble truths—suffering and its origin). Confusion about ultimate reality stems from being ignorant about the last two noble truths (path and cessation) or suchness—the way things truly are. Ignorance is taught as the first of the twelve links because the cycle of saṃsāra starts with the obscuration of perceiving how things are on the level of both seeming and ultimate reality. Or ignorance refers to the assumption that persons and phenomena really exist as well as to the clinging to that wrong idea.

The second link is "formation," which arises in dependence upon the previous link of ignorance. This link refers to the arising of the main mental afflictions of attachment, aversion, and bewilderment, which are caused by the ignorance described in the first link, as well as the production and accumulation of positive and negative karmas triggered by these afflictions. All of this depends on our habits, preferences, and fixations, which are rooted in ignorance. In this way, our karmic formations propel us into future rebirths in the desire realm, form realm, or formless realm. The places and specific qualities of these births result from the virtuous and nonvirtuous actions of our body, speech, and mind.

The third link is the particular kind of consciousness that contains the sum of certain karmic formations or imprints which cause it to enter one of the six realms of saṃsāra in accordance with those imprints. Once this consciousness has entered its new existence, such as a human being conceived in a womb, the full five skandhas develop, which are indicated by the fourth link of "name and form." "Name" refers to the four mental skandhas since they lack form and can only be named but cannot be shown to the senses.

In that process of developing the skandhas, we also develop our six senses (the six inner āyatanas), which is the fifth link. This leads to the next link of making contact with objects. Such contact produces feelings, which lead to craving—both craving to enjoy pleasant feelings and craving to avoid or get rid of unpleasant feelings. Craving can show up as either wanting to have something or wanting to get rid of something, but it is wanting in both cases. Craving leads to grasping—if we really want something, we reach out for it. Grasping develops into "becoming," that is, solidification. The more we grasp at something, the more we solidify it, which in this case means that we end up with a new birth. This process is similar to seeing the latest fancy computer, having pleasant feelings about it, wanting to have it, actually buying it, and then surfing the internet with it. But from that moment onward, aging starts, which means that, at the moment we bring home that computer, it is already outdated. Likewise, our five skandhas are already outdated the very moment we assume them, that is, the process of aging does not start around forty or fifty, but at the moment of conception in the womb. The final result of that process is the disintegration of the skandhas, that is, death. Then, we are back to square one, which is ignorance, and it starts all over again. This means that there is no end to those twelve links, they are not a linear sequence, but a vicious circle, which is what the word "saṃsāra" means.

From the perspective of the prajñāpāramitā sūtras, the twelve links of dependent origination just represent further characteristics to let go of, despite having to work with them temporarily on the path (as the sūtra said before, all phenomena are "without characteristics"). The twelve links say that saṃsāra is like a house of cards built on ignorance. The foundation, or bottom row of cards of this house, is ignorance and the rest of our saṃsāric house of cards is built on this ignorance. Once we pull out the bottom cards, the whole house collapses, which is the basic idea of using the twelve links as a means for liberation. Once we see that ignorance does not really exist, all the other links just collapse naturally. In this way, the regular order of the twelve links represents the characteristic of upholding saṃsāra, while their reverse order represents the characteristic of purification.

The Demise of the Four Noble Truths

Next the sūtra takes on the four noble truths:

> no suffering, no origin, no cessation, no path . . .

The *Heart Sūtra's* assault on Buddhist holy cows continues—the four noble truths do not really exist either. Of course, we can imagine that statements like that are shocking to many Buddhists. The prajñāpāramitā sūtras basically say, "There is no suffering, no causes of suffering, no cessation of suffering, and no path that leads to the cessation of suffering either. Still, try your best. You don't have a chance, but use it." That is bodhisattva logic, so to speak. As long as we do not really look into what all those things such as the four noble truths really are, they seem to exist and function, but as soon as we take a deeper look we cannot really find any of them.

At the same time, while looking at all of that, it is important not to get stuck on just the object side, that is, being overly involved in objectifying all those phenomena and meanwhile forgetting about our mind, which is the one who objectifies and also the one who can drop this objectifying. All phenomena become causes for suffering or causes for liberation only in dependence on how our mind deals with them. That is the bottom line—the *Heart Sūtra* is not primarily about all phenomena (be they skandhas or the four noble truths) as objects, but it is always pointing back to our mind as the subject and how it deals with all these objects. How do we deal with our eyes, our ears, our nose, our tongue, and our body? How do we deal with our sense perceptions? How do we deal with our suffering? How do we deal with the causes of our suffering? How do we deal with our path? As long as there is any solidifying of the path and its methods the path will not liberate us. It still may do some good, but it is limited and conditioned and not the full deal of liberation and omniscience.

The prajñāpāramitā sūtras keep reminding bodhisattvas of that at every turn, saying, "This is what you need to achieve through not fixating on it. But now that you have accomplished this great achievement, move on. Do not get stuck on it, do not hold on to it." On the bodhisattva path there are many stages of actually realizing something, such as directly seeing the true nature of phenomena on the first bhūmi. However, there is still some danger of making this realization into a trip. Of course, these bodhisattva trips are not as outrageous as our trips, but they may still have some tendencies of arrogance or feeling that they have something that others do not have. That is why these sūtras constantly warn, "Do not get inflated by anything, not even by your lack of being inflated." In this way, emptiness and the prajñā that realizes it are the safeguard of the bodhisattva path, being the sword that punctures the balloon of ego-inflation.

From the mahāyāna point of view, the four noble truths are nothing but further characteristics. The truth of suffering is the characteristic of being afflicted. The origin of suffering is the characteristic of appropriation, which means that we appropriate the five skandhas as that which is afflicted through its causes. The truth of the origin of suffering consists of karma and afflictions and those attract or appropriate new skandhas, and they do so not only from one lifetime to the next but also in every moment. We literally recreate our existence in every moment. Our life and our experiences not only depend on what we did in our last life or five days ago, but also on what happened in the immediately preceding moment. This is also going into the mix of the causes and conditions that make up the new mix of skandhas in the next moment. The truth of cessation has the characteristic of peace, that is, the lack of affliction. The path has the characteristic of prajñā, that is, insight or realization.

How do we understand these four noble truths from the mahāyāna point of view? The truth of suffering here means to understand how the skandhas are empty of suffering, which is the exact opposite of the original teaching, which says that the skandhas *are* suffering. In Buddhism usually suffering consists of the five skandhas, but in the mahāyāna the first noble truth means to see how the skandhas are empty of suffering because they are empty of nature, as the *Heart Sūtra* says at the beginning when Avalokiteśvara saw the five skandhas to be empty of nature. Since they are empty of nature, they are naturally empty of suffering, or anything else for that matter, including themselves. So when we wonder what is true in terms of the four noble truths, from the mahāyāna point of view, to say that the five skandhas are suffering is only a relative truth, but not the ultimate truth about the skandhas. When we look at the true nature of the five skandhas, we see that they are actually neither suffering nor anything else.

As for the origin of suffering, from a mahāyāna point of view it means not to grasp at and superimpose the causes of suffering. Usually it is said that the origin of suffering consists of karma and afflictions, which are taken to be really existent, whereas here we let go of the notion of actions and afflictions being the causes of suffering. We do not impose onto them that they really have the nature of being the causes of suffering. Ordinarily in the mahāyāna, the primary causes of suffering are attachment and wrong views—being confused and then being attached to what we are confused about, with these two reinforcing each other constantly. In fact, it is much easier to be attached to what one is confused about than to what one sees clearly.

As for the truth of cessation, ordinarily the notion of peace means that there was previously suffering and then it was brought to an end. However, the nature of cessation here in the mahāyāna means to understand that the skandhas never arise in the first place, do not abide in the present, and do not cease some time later. In other words, cessation means that, ultimately, nothing ever happens.

Finally, from the mahāyāna point of view, the truth of the path means to rest in meditative equipoise in nondual wisdom and realize the four noble truths to be emptiness, which includes the emptiness of that very nondual wisdom. Just as any other phenomenon, the path is not taken to be something substantial or some real entity, but as being empty. Still, the sūtras say that we need to travel it. However, the whole idea of traveling here is that there is no one to travel, no path, no vehicle, and no goal either.

No Hope in Prajñāpāramitā Either

However, if we think we can at least rely on the prajñā that realizes all this, the *Heart Sūtra* has no mercy with that either, saying:

> no wisdom, no attainment, and no nonattainment.

Even the very heart of the *Heart Sūtra*—prajñāpāramitā, which is nonconceptual and nondual wisdom—does not really exist. There is no prajñā and thus no prajñāpāramitā, which is the supreme culmination of prajñā. Conventionally speaking, wisdom is the fruition or an attainment, but strictly speaking it is just a name for the absence of ignorance. So if we see that there is no really existing ignorance in the first place, there is no lack of ignorance or realization either. In particular, here "wisdom" refers to the nondual wisdom of having relinquished all afflictive and cognitive obscurations, which means to know all phenomena without being attached to any of them or being obstructed with regard to any of them. Therefore, wisdom means the omniscience of a buddha, whose perception of all phenomena is completely unhindered, but lacks any sense of ownership or clinging to what it perceives. However, even that wisdom is no exception to being empty.

Needless to say, without a path and a fruition (nonconceptual wisdom or buddhahood), there cannot be any attainment of anything. Here "attainment" refers to the unsurpassable enlightenment of buddhahood with all its qualities (such as the ten powers and the four fearlessnesses). However, ultimately, this enlightenment cannot be attained because buddha wisdom is not identifiable as buddha wisdom. But if we finally give up and settle on that there is nothing to be attained at all, that is not it either, because there is also "no nonattainment."

"Nonattainment" can be understood to mean that buddha enlightenment is not yet attained by sentient beings. Or, usually, when we talk about attainment, we mean there is something that was not there before and that has been attained or newly acquired. Thus "nonattainment" can also mean that there is no such newly attained thing that did not exist before. If buddhahood were like that, it would be something conditioned. If it did not exist before and then came into being later, it would be impermanent and thus perish sooner or later. "No attainment" can also mean that since buddha nature abides equally in all sentient beings, there is no attainment because anything that could be attained in terms of buddhahood is already present in our mind. Buddha nature is not absent in the beginning and then attained at the end.

But on the other hand, this does not mean that there is no attainment at all either because from the perspective of the path it seems as if something is attained. This means that when the nature of the mind becomes manifest and realized as it is, from the point of view of confusion it seems that there is a change in terms of first not having seen this nature and then seeing it. But if we ask the nature of our mind, "Did you see any change?"—the answer is no. Therefore, it depends on whom we ask. If we ask ignorance, there is suffering, there is affliction, there is a path, and there is a fruition, but if we ask our buddha nature, none of these really exist. Thus, in Buddhism it is not just about asking the right questions, but it is also about whom we ask. Even if we ask the right question, but we ask our ignorant mind, it will still not be good enough. The final answer can only come from our wisdom mind.

From the point of view of buddha nature, when we talk about the five paths and the ten bhūmis, there is no real increase in qualities nor any decrease in flaws. The paths and bhūmis are simply a gradual process of unraveling the nature of the mind through the progressive purification or disappearance of the latent tendencies of ignorance—the ālaya-consciousness. This process culminates in the manifestation of the pure dharmadhātu as mirrorlike wisdom. From the point of view of ignorance, it seems as if there is some change or some progress. For example, when the sun is covered by clouds and then they gradually disappear, we can see the sun more and more. So if we ask the beings underneath the clouds, they will say that there is a change in terms of the sun being there or not being there. But if we ask the sun, there is no such change whatsoever. Likewise, from the perspective of the nature of the mind or the dharmadhātu, there is no change in terms of this nature increasing. From the point of view of the dharmadhātu, there is neither attainment nor nonattainment. In any case, no matter how we understand "nonattainment" here, it is empty too.

This last one is interesting because up to now we were in the mode of always saying, "No, no, no," and then suddenly the sūtra says that there is no nonattainment either. We can see our mind really getting into that mode of just saying "no" to everything, which tends toward the extreme of nihilism or just denying everything. But then that very denial is denied too. Of course, this does not mean that we just go back to where we started, taking back all the "no's" that we said. We are not going back, but we are not going further either. That is why "nonattainment" can also be understood as no training for anything to be attained. We do not reach some further attainment beyond "no attainment" that is "no nonattainment," thinking that this is the actual attainment. It means to watch the mind going more and more to one extreme, pulling out all the carpets under our feet (as well as our own feet) until we are steeped in the extreme of negation. And once we have settled into that state of mind of having negated everything and we think, "Okay, I got it now," the sūtra pulls out that last "non" carpet too. What happens then is that we drop, because this was the last carpet, so to speak. We just keep falling into groundlessness.

At that time, there is not even any cliff from which we drop, no surroundings to look at while we fall, nor any place where we might land. We are left with nothing but our experience of falling. How does our mind feel when there are no more carpets to stand on and nothing to land on? This falling into groundlessness is a weird kind of falling because we do not really fall anywhere and there is no one who is falling. It is falling without moving—we fall by staying in the same spot, which is the present moment of our experience. That is, our mind stays put where it is and just as it is and experiences fully what that is like. But there is no further mention or description of that, which would defeat the purpose of the *Heart Sūtra*. Once we are at that point of all carpets being gone, even the flying ones and even the noncarpets, what can we say? Anything we would say would just be another carpet that provides some false sense of security, whereas the idea of the prajñāpāramitā sūtras is not to provide any security whatsoever.

Padma Karpo said here that when existence is negated, this does not mean that emptiness is nonexistence. If emptiness were just the negation of existence, it would be nothing but a nonimplicative negation, but that is not suitable because any negation is still just a conceptual object and not what is experienced by nonconceptual wisdom as the genuine nature of phenomena.

Question: This goes back to the bodhisattva path and how we can apply these teachings in daily life. I am thinking of a particular situation of having difficulties with someone, and the stuckness and solidity of the experience is very clear to me in terms of the other person having very fixed views about the dynamics of this situation. I do not have the skillful means or the wisdom to know what to do, other than just trying to be open, looking at my experience in every moment, and trusting that I have the resources to at least attempt to be open and helpful. But there is also this habitual pattern of wanting to fix it, do the right thing, and help somebody.

KB: Beyond the things to do that you mention, what we also need to look at is that to think somebody else has a rigid view is in itself a rigid view. Being open also means to take a closer look at our own view of the view of that other person, whether it is really that rigid, or where we bump into it. We need to see where and how their view is rigid for us personally because it might not be rigid for somebody else. Some third person might think, "Yeah, that is exactly how it is." Therefore, it is the "bump zone" that is interesting to investigate because any rigid view can only be rigid in comparison to something else, which is our own view or our own mind. So the interesting area of practice is where those two views meet and rub against each other. Complete and true openness means that there is nothing to rub against, even for the most rigid or aggressive view, because there is no resistance toward it and nothing for it to bump into. It is more like a missile flying through a vacuum—there is no target to hit anywhere. So having some sense of openness for the other person's rigid view to be there is part of being open. The more internal space we have the less rub there is.

The Transparent Vajra of Fearlessness

The sūtra continues:

> Therefore, Śāriputra, since bodhisattvas have no attainment, they abide by relying on prajñāpāramitā.

Most commentaries say that this passage signifies the last moment of the tenth bhūmi, which is called "the vajralike samādhi." This is the last moment before buddhahood. At this point, all reference points in the minds of bodhisattvas are utterly at peace and they cannot really try to grasp, realize, or attain anything. This samādhi is about *being* free from all reference points, not trying to *become* free from all reference points. The vajralike samādhi is so subtle that anything we would try to do in it would prevent us from becoming a buddha. No matter what meditation technique or remedy we might apply at this point, it would just become an obstacle and a further obscuration. This means that at this point we completely let go of the last straw of both what is to be relinquished and its remedies. Despite its name, the vajralike samādhi is not really an active effort of cutting through the last thread of the rope that binds us, but it is about settling within the nature of the mind as it is, without any expectations or fears. Usually, when we talk about a vajra, it represents something very hard and indestructible, but there are two types of indestructibility. "Vajra" can refer to the hardest substance possible, which cannot be destroyed by anything, but is the most powerful weapon that destroys everything else. However, the vajralike samādhi is indestructible because there is absolutely nothing in it that provides any chance for being attacked or destroyed. It is the final realization that both the factors to be relinquished and their remedies are equally nonexistent. That is the supreme realization and we can forget about all antidotes, manipulations, purifications, improvements, or anything else to be done. It is due to its utter transparency and unobstructiveness that this samādhi is indestructible, just like space. Space is not hard and solid at all, but it is still indestructible because there is nothing in it that can be attacked.

This samādhi is also the final point of the view, meditation, and fruition being truly inseparable. The view is the view of emptiness free from any reference points. Meditation means to not just understand that emptiness or to realize half or three quarters of it, but to finally fully *be* that emptiness. In other words, in one's experience there is no difference between the freedom from reference points and the realization of the freedom from reference points. It is not just a concept or a fact, but that is what our mind *is* at that point. This is why it is indestructible. In Mahāmudrā terms, the vajralike samādhi means to rest in ordinary mind. More precisely, it is not just resting in it, which is still somewhat dualistic, but it refers to mind *being* ordinary mind, mind being itself, mind being at home and free in its own space. The Tibetan word for "meditation" means to familiarize, that is, to familiarize with the view. Thus, the final point of familiarization is to become or embody that with which we have ourselves familiarized. There is no difference between what we have familiarized with and the familiarizer. Therefore, view and meditation are finally completely undifferentiable.

Next the sūtra says:

Since their minds are without obscuration, they have no fear.

In the meditative equipoise of bodhisattvas on the bhūmis, there is no longer any obscuration and they are like a buddha in their realization. However, when they rise from their formal meditation session, they are not like a buddha because they cannot fully sustain their realization in every situation outside of their meditation. Therefore, the ten bhūmis consist of training in bringing the realization during meditative equipoise into any situation that one might encounter. During the periods between the meditation sessions of these bodhisattvas, all kinds of dualistic appearances still appear. However, the difference between them and us is not only that these appearances appear like illusions, but that bodhisattvas instantly realize them to be illusions—they do not get caught up in them anymore. Therefore, illusory bodhisattvas engage in illusory conduct for illusory beings with illusory objects, which is the reason why the state of mind of these bodhisattvas outside of their meditative equipoise of directly realizing emptiness is called "illusionlike samādhi." In this way, for bodhisattvas there is not even what we call "postmeditation" (which sounds like a break) because their "postmeditation" is simply another kind of samādhi, from within which they perform all kinds of altruistic conduct. This is samādhi in action, during which bodhisattvas integrate their realization into anything they do. We always try to do that and mostly fail, but bodhisattvas do it constantly.

The only obscurations during the times when bodhisattvas are not in formal meditation are a slight sense of characteristics and a slight sense of duality, but there is no clinging to real existence anymore on the bhūmis. As for clinging to characteristics, for example, when we have a dream and we wake up, we can talk about and label the dream appearances, such as someone in the dream having brown hair and blue eyes. We apply such characteristics, but we know perfectly well that what we apply them to does not really exist. Still, there is some degree of reifying appearances through ascribing characteristics to them. Likewise, during the first seven bhūmis, bodhisattvas know clearly and at all times that whatever appears does not really exist, but they still label illusory appearances. Up through the final moment of the tenth bhūmi there is also a slight sense of duality, experiencing a difference between subject and object. For the sense perception of bodhisattvas, for example, it still appears as if objects are outside, though they are fully aware of their not being outside. This is very different from our perception because we not only think that objects exist outside, but that they are real and also that the perceiver is real. Finally, at buddhahood there are no more such obscurations during "postmeditation" at all, which means that there is no more difference between "meditation" and "postmeditation." In other words, this is the complete union of meditation and conduct.

Maybe in these modern times the most essential message of the *Heart Sūtra* is to say that "bodhisattvas have no fear." With people feeling separated from the world and other people, fear about everything seems to be the main problem in the world these days. Of course, there is fear about bad things, but there is also fear about good things (such as fear about love), and even fear about fear. There is literally nothing that some people are not afraid of. So why is there no fear in bodhisattvas and buddhas? It corresponds to the statement in the *lojong* ("mind training") teachings that "the supreme protection is emptiness." The more walls we try to build or the more fending-off techniques we try to employ, the more our fears increase, as we can witness so dramatically in many places in the world. No matter how high we build the walls and fences that keep people out, we just get more paranoid.

We have talked about the ice and water example before. On the path, when we start with a big ice chunk of saṃsāric existence or our five skandhas, it is cold, hard, sharp, and jagged, and we can easily cut ourselves. Unlike water, it is not gentle, fluid, and yielding. Our job on the path is to melt down this ice chunk of saṃsāra, and the more ice we melt, the more water we have. That water, besides having the quality of being the result of having melted ice, also has the quality of enhancing the process of ice melting itself. If we have a big chunk of ice and just let it sit there in a sink, it takes a long time, but if we plug the sink's drain so the ice melt surrounds the ice, the ice melts quicker. In that way, the melted water is a catalyst for melting the ice. Likewise, progress on the path and the dissolution of afflictions and obscurations are somewhat slow in the beginning. Our rigid views and habitual patterns first soften up, just as ice softens before it turns into actual water, and what they melt into is the water of emptiness and compassion. The more we have of that water, the quicker our remaining obscurations melt.

Now, once we see the lack of real existence of both the factors to be relinquished and their antidotes, there is an increasing sense of fearlessness. When we realize that there is really nothing to be hurt, and nothing that hurts us, there is no ground for fear. This is called "the samādhi of a hero's stride," which is another samādhi described in the sūtras. In a general sense this means that bodhisattvas progress fearlessly through the bhūmis. Not only do they perceive everything as illusory, be it good or bad, beneficial or harmful, but there is an increasing sense of self-confidence. This is not self-confidence in the usual sense of being a hero, such as having massive muscles, overwhelming firepower, bulletproof vests, and so on, but it is confidence in our own transparency and the transparency of any situation in which we find ourselves. This means increasing confidence in our ability to cope with anybody and any situation in the most beneficial way. The more transparent we and any situation around us become, the less we have to have fixed plans for worst-case scenarios, and the more our natural creativity for problem-solving increases because we are more able to see what is actually going on and act accordingly.

Usually we think we have to have a thousand different plans for a thousand different scenarios to cover all bases, but what about scenario one thousand and one? Then we freak out and do not know what to do because we have no ready-made plan. We feel we have to go back to our think tank and figure out another plan before we can deal with that unexpected person or situation. This approach is obviously limited, conditional, and dualistic. The idea of fearlessness here is to chuck out all our plans and strategies, no matter how good they seem, to rely solely on being comfortable within the fundamental groundlessness of our being, and then to act out of this spaciousness. Within that space there is enough room for the right thing to happen. Especially in the Tibetan tradition, not to have a plan is a good idea. No matter what plan we have, it is not going to work out anyway, which seems to be the overall big plan.

In general, we could say that fear comes from clinging to the opposites of the Buddhist "four seals" (i.e., clinging to "the four mistaken views"). The four seals say:

Everything conditioned is impermanent.
Everything contaminated is suffering.
All phenomena are empty and without a self.
Only nirvāṇa is peace.

We usually cling to the permanence of conditioned phenomena, regard contaminated phenomena (those produced by afflictions and karma) as happiness, take phenomena to be really existent and having a nature of their own, and seek peace in saṃsāra. All of that causes fear, which is just another word for the fundamental experience of suffering—fear of not getting or losing what we want and fear of getting what we do not want. In this sense, fear means to have no control over what will happen next. In fact, even with all our plans and safety measures, we never know what will happen in the next moment.

Similarly, in terms of "the four mistaken views," ordinary beings cling to their bodies as being pure, at least more or less. We do not usually meditate on our bodies being made up of all kinds of completely filthy substances, as is done in the meditation on the repulsiveness of the body. We also cling to our feelings as being happiness. No matter what feelings we have, even in negative or painful ones, there is some sense of the juiciness of our existence. Even if we feel bad, at least we feel alive somehow, rather than having no feelings. Next, we cling to our mind as being our self in one sense or the other. Finally, we cling to all phenomena as being permanent, not necessarily forever, but we do think that things last for a certain amount of time without changing. We certainly do not think of phenomena as being impermanent in the sense of literally changing moment by moment.

In current events we can easily see how fear is produced and increased through solidifying certain persons, situations, countries, or ethnic or religious groups. It is like solidifying our own dream, like desperately trying not to wake up and often even making the dream worse, like deliberately having nightmares all the time. In brief, the more we solidify persons and things the more real they become, and the more fearful they can become. To realize that things are not as solid as they seem radically reduces our fearfulness, even if we only get a little bit of a different perspective. That does not necessarily mean to realize emptiness, but just to have some more space in our minds and to relax. We could say that lack of mental space means an increase in fear, while increase in mental space equals a decrease in fear. When we finally directly see the illusory nature of all our manipulative thoughts and actions regarding solidified phenomena in saṃsāra, this is called the realization of emptiness.

Arriving at Dwelling Nowhere

The sūtra continues:

> Having fully transcended delusion, they attain complete nirvāṇa.

One interpretation of bodhisattvas having completely gone beyond any kind of delusion is that the dharmakāya—the fruition of buddhahood—is without any flaws or mistakes. Or delusion refers to investing in real existence and seeing phenomena as real. In other words, it means to see the unmistaken reality in a mistaken manner, just like mistaking a garden hose for a snake. It can also mean that bodhisattvas (from the path of seeing onward) and buddhas have awakened from the sleep of ignorance. To "attain complete nirvāṇa" can be understood as referring to the two form kāyas as the natural outflow of the dharmakāya (indicated by "having fully transcended delusion"), which represent the aspects of buddhahood—the invisible and intangible dharmakāya—that are visible and tangible for other beings. The way in which buddhas display themselves to other beings and instruct and benefit them is through the form kāyas. "Complete nirvāṇa" also refers to the nonabiding nirvāṇa of the mahāyāna. Through their prajñā buddhas do not abide in saṃsāra, but, through their great compassion, they also do not abide in nirvāṇa in the sense of hanging out in their private penthouse with all the amenities and a nice view of saṃsāra, without being involved in it anymore.

Furthermore, "complete nirvāṇa" means that buddhas have not only awakened from their sleep of ignorance, but have also extended their mind towards all phenomena, thus being omniscient. Two of the main meanings of the word "buddha" are "to awake," which is why the Buddha is often called "the awakened one," and "to unfold," just as the bud of a lotus flower unfolds. We can also understand this as our mind having been contracted in saṃsāra like a tight fist, and nirvāṇa meaning to let go and uncurl that fist. The nature of the mind, even within the tight fist of confused, dualistic, and paranoid mind, is always just as it is, but nirvāṇa means that mind's nature finally has the space to fully unfold itself and be itself in its entire openness and vividness. We can also say that the complete nirvāṇa at the end of the bodhisattva path means simply returning to the natural nirvāṇa, which is nothing other than natural emptiness or the nature of all phenomena. The final realization is an experience in which emptiness just *is* as opposed to being something that is realized by somebody (such as a buddha) or something (such as nonconceptual wisdom).

Next the sūtra says:

> All the buddhas who abide in the three times fully awaken to unsurpassable completely perfect enlightenment by relying on prajñāpāramitā.

After the sūtra has made it clear that ultimately there is neither attainment nor nonattainment, it says here that, from the relative or seeming point of view of the path, bodhisattvas attain complete nirvāṇa and awaken to unsurpassable enlightenment. Relatively speaking, there is the attainment of nirvāṇa and buddhahood as long as we do not reify it and fixate on it. In other words, as long as we want to attain something or strive for something, there is no real attainment. Once we let go of wanting, striving, and goal orientation, and just engage in bodhisattva activity for the welfare of others without any self-concern, enlightenment or buddhahood will happen naturally. In other words, buddhahood is really nothing but a by-product of the bodhisattva path, since the main objective and function of that path is to help all sentient beings to gain freedom from suffering, not to attain buddhahood for one's own sake. Therefore, we cannot really *attain* buddhahood, but we can let it happen. The means to dispel all the obscurations that prevent buddhahood from taking place is prajñāpāramitā and this is why it is said to be the mother of all buddhas. If we familiarize with emptiness through prajñāpāramitā, the outcome is to wake up from our sleep of ignorance. Therefore, the sūtra says that all the buddhas of the three times, through prajñāpāramitā, fully awaken to enlightenment.

As mentioned before, prajñāpāramitā is both the means and the result since buddhahood is the ultimate perfection of prajñā (prajñāpāramitā), which is nonconceptual and nondual buddha wisdom. In this way, prajñā functions very much in the same way as water in the example of ice melting into water. As mentioned before, the result of ice having melted is water, but this water is actively involved in the process of further melting the remaining ice. Likewise, prajñāpāramitā or our buddha nature, the nature of our mind, is not some kind of inert, neutral, and inactive thing or like a shy sleeping beauty who is waiting to be discovered by us. It gives us wake-up calls all the time, but usually we just ignore them. If we let our buddha nature's wake-up calls get through to us and do not hit the snooze button again and again, eventually we will wake up fully and enjoy our ride in the bright daylight of nondual wisdom within the vast sky of mind's spaciousness.

To summarize all of this in terms of view, meditation, conduct, and fruition, the view is that there is no arising and no ceasing upon freeing ourselves through not observing any afflicted or purified phenomena. Meditation means to rest in just that, which is inconceivable emptiness. When we talk about the view here, it is not really an object of conceptual mind, though that is how we start out. The actual view refers to the first genuine experience of emptiness or the nature of the mind. Then we really know what we are talking about, but before that emptiness is just a more or less vague concept. The view means to actually see what the prajñāpāramitā sūtras are talking about because it is only then that we can really familiarize ourselves with it. If we have no clear and direct experience of what it is, we are just becoming familiar with some more or less vague idea. In the Dzogchen and Mahāmudrā traditions this is what pointing-out instructions refer to. The view in Dzogchen and Mahāmudrā is not something that we establish through conceptual analysis, but it needs to be experienced directly. "Ordinary mind" in Mahāmudrā or "awareness" (*rigpa*) in Dzogchen refers to the experience of mind's nature. Thus, meditation means to familiarize with that experience and sustain it, making it gapless. When we experience mind's nature, we have a gap in our experience of deluded dualistic mind. This is the "good" kind of gap, and then we train in making that gap experience gapless, without any "bad" gaps of not being in *rigpa*, which is ignorance (*marigpa* in Tibetan).

Then conduct just means not to be separated from that experience of *rigpa* no matter what we do. This does not really add anything to the view and meditation; the point is simply to carry the view and meditation over into whatever physical and verbal actions we engage in. In more technical terms, conduct means to repeatedly review the meaning of the heart of the Buddha's teachings and thus never be separated from emptiness. Very often people wonder how to apply the dharma in their everyday life. A lot of people hear all kinds of teachings on emptiness, buddha nature, Mahāmudrā, and Dzogchen, and after twenty or thirty years they still ask, "How do I apply the dharma in my everyday life?" They are still looking for something else over and above all these teachings, some kind of trick or five-point plan for all kinds of situations in their life. "What do I do if I have problems with my boss?" "What do I do if I have problems with my spouse?" "What do I do if I have problems with my dog?" We are always looking for detailed prescriptions for each and every situation, somehow thinking that our dharma life on the cushion and in the shrine room is different from everything else we do. But the actual way to apply the dharma in everyday life is to mix the view and meditation with whatever we encounter and engage in, which means to connect with the experience of the nature of the mind in every situation. That is the plan, which is obviously not really a plan. This perhaps explains why planning-oriented Western minds often are not magnetized by the simple notion of mixing our view and meditation with anything we encounter as being sophisticated advice for "dharma in everyday life."

Finally, the fruition of all this is to have succeeded in bringing the view and meditation into every possible (and impossible) situation. There is no difference anymore between meditation and nonmeditation, meditation and conduct, or our dharmic life and our everyday life. In more technical terms, buddhas have no object of their wisdom mind and sentient beings have no object of consciousness. Also, neither nonconceptual wisdom nor the stains of knowable objects exist. Therefore, there is nothing to be attained and nothing to be lost.

The Mantra—The Final Leap off the Cliff

This finishes the teaching part proper of the *Heart Sūtra*. Next we come to the mantra of prajñāpāramitā:

> Therefore, the great mantra of prajñāpāramitā, the mantra of great insight, the unsurpassed mantra, the mantra equal to the unequaled, the mantra that calms all suffering, should be known to be true since it is undeceiving.

Though mantras usually pertain to the vajrayāna, there are a number of sūtras in which mantras appear. Literally, "mantra" means "mind protection." *Man* is an abbreviation of *manas* (one of the many Sanskrit words for "mind") and *tra* or *traya* means "protection." One way to interpret this is that mind's nature is protected from adventitious stains, afflictions, and obscurations. Or *man* stands for *prajñā*, while *tra* is compassion or skill in means, so *mantra* refers to the union of prajñā and compassion, with the two syllables *man* and *tra* being the natural outflow of these two. Therefore, the actual mantra is the inseparability of prajñā and compassion. It is said that great bodhisattvas and buddhas can bless syllables to have a certain effectiveness. They do so through their mind being in samādhi, not through sprinkling holy water on the syllables or something like that. Thus, the syllables of the mantra represent a natural outflow or outcome of that samādhi. In this way the actual mantra is a state of samādhi, basically resting in the nature of the mind, which is the ultimate unity of prajñā and compassion. This is not only symbolized by certain syllables, but these syllables are "charged" with the beneficial energy of samādhi, thus being the nominal mantra. Here, since the realization of emptiness is so powerful, it is like a mantra in that it protects the mind from dualistic projections and reference points.

This mantra of prajñāpāramitā is "great" because it dispels all inner and outer hindrances. As for its being "the mantra of great insight," literally, the Sanskrit for "insight" is *vidyā* (Tibetan *rigpa*), which means "knowledge" and is the opposite of ignorance (*avidyā* or *marigpa*). It is the mantra of great insight, or the *vidyāmantra*, because it overcomes the delusion of any solid external reality. Or it is so called because it dispels ignorance and produces insight or wisdom, eliminating *avidyā* and giving rise to *vidyā*. It is also said to be "the unsurpassed mantra" because it overcomes all delusion about any solid reality on both the external and the internal level. Or it is unsurpassable because it means being free from the three spheres of agent, object, and action.

As for this mantra being "equal to the unequaled," "the unequaled" is buddhahood, and emptiness is the mantra that is equal to the unequaled—buddhahood—because emptiness is able to bring sentient beings to buddhahood. Emptiness is the means to arrive at buddhahood and it is in that sense that it is like a mantra because mantras are used for certain purposes. This again highlights the fact that emptiness is not an end in itself, but a tool. Or the expression "equal to the unequaled" can be understood in the sense that the dharmakāyas of all buddhas are equal, while their form kāyas are not equal. Also, prajñāpāramitā is equal to the wisdom and enlightened activity of all buddhas, but not equal to the minds and deeds of ordinary beings, śrāvakas, and pratyekabuddhas.

The prajñāpāramitā mantra is also "the mantra that calms all suffering." Prajñāpāramitā does not only dispel suffering, but also the causes and conditions for suffering. Or prajñāpāramitā teaches the path to end all suffering. According to some commentaries, to recite the prajñāpāramitā sūtras, keep them in mind, learn them by heart, constantly recite them in our mind, and explain them to others eliminates all problems and diseases and brings us under the protection of buddhas and bodhisattvas. In other words, to practice prajñāpāramitā overturns the ocean of saṃsāra.

The mantra of prajñāpāramitā "should be known to be true since it is undeceiving." "Should be known" points to prajñāpāramitā as being the cause for attaining buddhahood. It is what we need to actively and personally cultivate and not just leave as letters on paper, but integrate it in our mind. Prajñāpāramitā is the sole ultimate "truth," or ultimate reality. In terms of the three doors to liberation, ultimately it is signless and true in terms of the body since it is not practiced with the body. It is wishless and true in terms of speech since it is not spoken with words. It is empty and true in terms of the mind since it is inconceivable for the mind. Unlike all other things, prajñāpāramitā (or emptiness) is true because it never leads to any form of deception and thus is the true path to buddhahood. The only thing for which we cannot use prajñāpāramitā (or emptiness) is to become more confused. If we become more confused, it is a sure sign that we did not work with emptiness, but something else. It is also said that prajñāpāramitā is undeceiving because it fulfills all our wishes, meaning those wishes in accord with the motivation and the path of bodhisattvas. It is also undeceiving because it cuts through doubts. As mentioned before, one of the main features of prajñā is to gain irreversible certainty about how things really are.

After these descriptions of the mantra of prajñāpāramitā, the sūtra spells out the mantra:

The prajñāpāramitā mantra is said as follows:

OM GATE GATE PĀRAGATE PĀRASAMGATE BODHI SVĀHĀ.

OM means nothing. OM means everything. OM means OM. It is often the first syllable of mantras and there are many volumes of explanations on what OM means in both Hinduism and Buddhism. Simply put, in Buddhism OM symbolizes and carries the blessings of all buddhas, serving as an auspicious beginning of a mantra in that this blessing dispels all ignorance and produces the fruition of great wisdom, or *rigpa*. OM can also be understood as the three vajras of enlightened body, speech, and mind since it is composed of the three Sanskrit letters A, U, and M.

The next two syllables—GATE GATE—literally mean "gone, gone." All reference points are gone with the wind of the prajñā of realizing emptiness. One commentary says that these two syllables symbolize the two meanings of *abhiṣeka* since this is a mantra. One meaning of *abhiṣeka* is "to dispel" and the other is "to pour" or "to sprinkle." This means that, through the mantra, we dispel obstacles, hindrances, and obscurations and instead pour wisdom into our being. In particular, the vase *abhiṣeka* is said to dispel obstacles, and when we drink the water in the vase, wisdom is poured into us, so to speak.

PĀRAGATE means "gone beyond," "gone to the other shore," or "gone to the other side." "Beyond" refers to the unsurpassable, which is prajñāpāramitā, emptiness, or enlightenment. Going or having gone there means to familiarize with the fundamental meaning of the prajñāpāramitā sūtras. In meditative equipoise such familiarization is spacelike in terms of resting in mind's vast openness without any reference points. In between meditation sessions bodhisattvas train in the various focal objects of prajñā, such as bodhicitta and the six pāramitās, which means to train in the illusionlike samādhi. This is how bodhisattvas go beyond—beyond saṃsāra, beyond ego-mind, and beyond dualism.

However, even that is not enough because PĀRASAṂGATE means "to go completely beyond"—we even go beyond "beyond." This means that the mere fact of having gone beyond saṃsāra also exists in śrāvakas and pratyekabuddhas, but where they end up is not sufficient for bodhisattvas because śrāvakas and pratyekabuddhas get stuck in their personal little nirvāṇa without being of further benefit to others. Bodhisattvas even go beyond that, which means they enter the nonabiding nirvāṇa. Thus, bodhisattvas go beyond all reference points and clinging with regard to both saṃsāra and nirvāṇa.

BODHI means "perfect realization," "the illuminated or enlightened mind," or "wisdom." Here it is said to represent the final state of buddhahood with its four kinds of enlightened activity—peaceful, enriching, magnetizing, and wrathful. SVĀHĀ literally means "may it be!" Thus, in a sense, it has the same meaning as "amen." So if we have been Christians and miss saying "amen" in Buddhism, we can just say SVĀHĀ instead. Thus, BODHI SVĀHĀ means "May there be enlightenment!" or "May enlightenment be!" This is where mind "arrives" once it has gone beyond "beyond"—the nondimensional "place" of no return. In buddhahood there is no return to saṃsāra, dualistic mind, or even the bodhisattva path. However, it is the final return to our fundamental nature, from which we had strayed for so long. In that way, it is like coming home after a long and tiresome journey through foreign lands.

Some also say that the prajñāpāramitā mantra summarizes the four key aspects of the view, the path, the conduct, and the fruition of the prajñāpāramitā sūtras, which consist of being illusionlike and the three doors to liberation (emptiness, signlessness, and wishlessness). In this sense, GATE GATE means that all mindfulness has gone to be illusionlike. On the path we start out with mindfulness (the first GATE) and then we let go of it (the second GATE). We do not really lose it, as mindfulness becomes much more powerful when we do not try to deliberately cultivate it, which entails a lot of effort, concepts, and dualism. When mindfulness becomes illusionlike, it has a lighter touch and is more natural, which is the idea here. We could call this "mind-less mindfulness." PĀRAGATE means that we have gone even beyond illusionlike mindfulness, which means having gone beyond to emptiness. PĀRASAMGATE refers to having gone beyond both illusionlike mindfulness and emptiness, which refers to having gone to signlessness, or the lack of any characteristics whatsoever, including emptiness. Finally, BODHI SVĀHĀ means having purified all afflictive and cognitive obscurations and thus having gone to wishlessness, or having gone beyond mind altogether (Tib. lodé; blo 'das). The latter expression is also often used in Mahāmudrā and Dzogchen. Śāntideva said the same in the ninth chapter of his Bodhicaryāvatāra:

The ultimate is not the sphere of cognition.[10]

"Mind" or "cognition" refers to dualistic mind, so we literally go out of our mind, that is, out of our dualistic mind. We step out of the ballpark of our dualistic mind and step into what mind actually is. Obviously this does not mean that we lose our mind at that point, drop dead, or dissolve

---

10   IX.2c.

into nothingness, but it means that we step out of our usual sphere of experience altogether—this is the end of the world as we know it.

The prajñāpāramitā mantra is also said to reflect the five paths. GATE GATE stands for the paths of accumulation and preparation. PĀRAGATE refers to the path of seeing. PĀRASAṂGATE symbolizes the path of meditation (or familiarization), and BODHI SVĀHĀ is the path of no more learning.

Atiśa gives an interesting comment here, saying that everything that is said in the sūtra before the mantra is for those of duller faculties, for whom the brief version of the sūtra's contents as condensed in the mantra remains secret. In other words, if we do not get what the *Heart Sūtra* is about via the mantra, we have to read through the entire sūtra, but for people of sharp faculties the mantra should be enough. This seems to be the reason why it is at the end of the sūtra.

When Avalokiteśvara finishes his teaching, he utters the mantra, which also signals a radical shift in terms of the didactic approach altogether. Despite the *Heart Sūtra*'s deconstructive approach, everything up through "All the buddhas who abide in the three times fully awaken to unsurpassable completely perfect enlightenment by relying on prajñāpāramitā"—the fourfold emptiness, the eightfold profundity, all the lists of no skandhas, no dhātus, no āyatanas, no dependent origination, no four noble truths, no wisdom, no attainment, and no nonattainment—is still analytical, conceptual, and dualistic, thus based on the rational mind. Up to that point the sūtra is still contemplative and there is at least some rudimentary content, but the mantra signifies a qualitative leap in our approach to the whole thing. The mantra marks the point where we are encouraged to leap into the nonrational and non-conceptual space of the direct experience of what the sūtra has been talking about so far. Avalokiteśvara has pushed us farther and farther toward the edge of the cliff through what he said so far, but the mantra is the final push over the edge because in terms of words or intellectual understanding there is nothing more to say or think at this point. The mantra encourages us to leap into the experience of *śūnyatā* without any concepts and without holding on to anything. In his commentary on the *Heart Sūtra*, Thich Nhat Hanh says:

When we listen to the mantra, we should bring ourselves into that state of attention, of concentration, so that we can receive the strengths emanated from Avalokiteśvara Bodhisattva. We do not recite the Heart Sūtra like singing a song or with our intellect alone. If you practice the meditation on emptiness, if you penetrate the nature of interbeing with all your heart, your body and your mind, you will realize a state that is quite concentrated. If you say the mantra then, with all your being, the mantra will have power, and you will be able to have real communication, real communion with Avalokiteśvara, and you will be able to transform yourself into the direction of enlightenment. So this text is not just for chanting, or to be put on the altar for worship. It is given to us as a tool to work for our liberation; for the liberation of all beings.[11]

Once we have gone through the sūtra using it as a contemplative manual, our arrival at the point of saying the mantra is quite different from just saying the mantra on its own because our mind is in a very different state, being charged by both the words of the sūtra and our mental focus on their meaning. We are in a samādhi situation here, having at least to some extent stripped our mind of its conceptual garments. When spoken from within that state of mind, the mantra has much greater power, which means that there is a better chance for us to actually leap off the cliff. Then we can read all the Cliff Notes; we just need to make sure that we fall slowly and enjoy the view.

In a sense, the mantra is like the punch line in a really good joke. If you just blurt out the punch line without leading up to it through the rest of the joke that precedes it, it does not make any sense and has no effect—no one will understand what it is about, let alone laugh. In a sense, the mantra is the final laugh about the cosmic joke of the *Heart Sūtra*. When we laugh really hard about a good joke, we do not think about the words that lead up to the punch line or even the punch line anymore, but we are in a nonconceptual space of enjoyment and letting go of any tension, just relishing the moment. Similarly, the mantra is like finally having grokked the eternal joke of saṃsāra and nirvāṇa.

11 Thich Nhat Hanh 1988, pp. 50–51.

The Buddha's Applause

Finally, we come to the conclusion of Avalokiteśvara's teaching:

> In this way, Śāriputra, bodhisattva mahāsattvas should train in the profound prajñāpāramitā.

Several commentators say that Avalokiteśvara's entire answer to Śāriputra can be divided into sections representing the five paths. According to Kamalaśīla, the paths of accumulation and preparation, which still rely on analytical and inferential knowledge, are represented by the passage "Noble Avalokiteśvara . . . In the same way, feeling, discrimination, formation, and consciousness are emptiness." The path of seeing consists of the eightfold profundity: "Thus, Śāriputra, all phenomena are emptiness . . . without decrease, and without increase." The path of familiarization is "Therefore, Śāriputra, in emptiness there is no form . . . Since their minds are without obscuration, they have no fear." The path of no more learning consists of "Having fully transcended delusion, they attain complete nirvāṇa" (the dharmakāya) and "All the buddhas who abide in the three times fully awaken to unsurpassable completely perfect enlightenment by relying on prajñāpāramitā" (the two form kāyas).

According to Padma Karpo, the passage "Noble Avalokiteśvara . . . In the same way, feeling, discrimination, formation, and consciousness are emptiness" represents the view, which is like looking in the direction of one's destination. "Thus, Śāriputra, all phenomena are emptiness . . . no attainment, and no nonattainment" indicates meditation, which is like walking toward one's destination. In particular, "Therefore, Śāriputra, since bodhisattvas have no attainment, they abide by relying on prajñāpāramitā. Since their minds are without obscuration, they have no fear" represents the vajralike samādhi as the final meditation. "Having fully transcended delusion . . . unsurpassable completely perfect enlightenment by relying on prajñāpāramitā" stands for the fruition, which is like having arrived at one's destination. "Therefore, the great mantra of prajñāpāramitā . . . OṂ GATE GATE PĀRAGATE PĀRASAṂGATE BODHI SVĀHĀ" points to conduct, which is the secret path of bodhisattvas.

Since Śāriputra asked in the beginning how a son or daughter of noble family should train in the profound prajñāpāramitā, Avalokiteśvara explained the way in which bodhisattvas travel on the path to buddhahood. Now the Buddha confirms that this is truly the way to go:

> Then the Bhagavān rose from that samādhi and spoke to noble Avalokiteśvara, the bodhisattva mahāsattva, "Well done! Good, good, O son of noble family. Thus it is, O son of noble family, thus it is."

At the beginning of the sūtra, the Buddha had entered "the samādhi of the perception of the profound," and now he is finally released from duty. Avalokiteśvara served as a perfect broadcaster for the Buddha's mind and took care of the job of answering Śāriputra's question, so the Buddha can go back to normal, so to speak. Not, however, without giving his explicit approval of what Avalokiteśvara has said. Basically the Buddha says that what Avalokiteśvara said is as good as what the Buddha himself could have said. Moreover, Avalokiteśvara is given the Buddha's stamp of full approval not just once, but twice. According to some commentaries, the first time of saying "Good, O son of noble family, thus it is" means that the Buddha approves Avalokiteśvara's presentation of the path, which is the causal aspect of prajñāpāramitā, while the second time of saying "Good, O son of noble family, thus it is" represents his approval of the fruitional aspect of prajñāpāramitā, which is buddhahood. In the sūtra, everything from "O Śāriputra, a son of noble family or a daughter of noble family . . . should see in this way . . ." up through ". . . they have no fear" represents the path, while "All the buddhas who abide in the three times fully awaken to unsurpassable completely perfect enlightenment by relying on prajñāpāramitā" refers to the fruition. When the Buddha says, "Thus it is," he refers to the mind being completely freed once profound reality is realized, which is mind's natural "thusness" that was never other or tainted by anything.

The Buddha concludes:

> "One should practice the profound prajñāpāramitā just as you have taught and the tathāgatas will rejoice."

This is the final guarantee of the Buddha—if we practice prajñā-pāramitā as Avalokiteśvara explained, there is no way not to become a buddha. In addition, we get the added bonus of making all buddhas happy. However, of course, the main point of practicing the bodhisattva path is to make all beings happy, not so much the buddhas (being buddhas, they are already happy). The fact that bodhisattvas make all beings happy is the reason why the buddhas praise and rejoice in all the activities of bodhisattvas, and this bodhisattva activity of benefiting beings is at the same time the best way to make the buddhas happy.

The Epilogue

The remaing part of the sūtra consists of the epilogue (or the conclusion), which is common to all prajñāpāramitā sūtras:

> When the Bhagavān had said this, venerable Śāriputra and noble Avalokiteśvara, the bodhisattva mahāsattva, all those surrounding them, and the world with its gods, humans, asuras, and gandharvas rejoiced and praised the words of the Bhagavān.

Though the Buddha did not say much, the entire sūtra bears the authority of his speech. The introduction of the sūtra only speaks of humans—monastics and bodhisattvas—as its audience, but obviously there were many other beings too, such as all kinds of gods. Asuras are the demigods within the six realms of saṃsāra who always fight with the gods about a huge miraculous tree with the most delicious fruits. The roots of this tree are in the asura realm, but the branches with the fruits grow in the god realm—we all know how those disputes about some branches of the trees in our garden growing into our neighbor's garden end. Gandharvas are the celestial musicians who play for the gods and live only on smells. Must be all those dead rock musicians who just keep playing on their "cloud number nine"! That all of these beings "rejoiced and praised the words of the Bhagavān" means not only that they praised and rejoiced in the Buddha's actual spoken words at the end of the sūtra, but this also refers to everything that Avalokiteśvara had said through the power of the Buddha's blessings while in samādhi.

A Meditation on Prajñāpāramitā and the *Heart Sūtra*

As for practicing more with prajñāpāramitā, the Tibetan canon of the Indian Buddhist treatises (*Tengyur*) contains a brief sādhana by a siddha named Dārika which represents an internal reenactment of the *Heart Sūtra*. The following is an abbreviated version of this sādhana and its visualization.[12]

We start the meditation with imagining that from the syllable MAM standing on a lotus and sun disk in our heart light radiates out and invites all buddhas and bodhisattvas to the space in front of us. In their presence we go for refuge to the three jewels, give rise to bodhicitta, and cultivate the four immeasurables of love, compassion, joy, and equanimity. Then we say the emptiness mantra OM SVABHĀVA ŚUDDHA SARVA DHARMA SVABHĀVA ŚUDDHO 'HAM. Literally, this means "OM, all phenomena are pure by nature and pure by nature am I." It refers to everything internal and external being naturally empty. Often sādhanas say after this mantra that everything becomes emptiness, which is usually misconceived as things not having been empty before and then becoming or being made empty. This sādhana is one of the few that explicitly tells us to contemplate that everything is primordially emptiness by nature. The mantra does not mean to imagine that everything dissolves into nothingness or to close our eyes and pretend that nothing is there, but it means to bring to mind the fact that everything always has been and

---

12 For more details, see Lopez 1988, pp. 114–19.

will be empty by nature. Thus, the main thing is not the mantra, but the contemplation of the natural emptiness of all phenomena.

Out of this state of natural emptiness those who are familiar with the visualization of the four elements, Mount Meru, and on top of that a beautiful palace with a throne supported by eight lions, a lotus, and a sun disk can build up the visualization in that way. Those who are not familiar with it can just visualize a lion throne in space, on top of which there is an open lotus flower and a sun disk lying within the lotus. On the sun disk we visualize ourselves as Prajñāpāramitā. We simply forget about our ordinary body and mind, replacing ourselves with Prajñāpāramitā, who is yellow in color, with four arms and all the ornaments of a sambhogakāya form. In the visualization in this sādhana she does not hold a sword in her upper right hand, but a vajra. Her upper left hand holds a scripture. The lower two hands are usually in the meditation gesture, but in this sādhana the lower right hand is in the gesture of protection (the wrist resting on her right knee, with the palm facing upward and outward). The lower left hand is in the mudrā of teaching the dharma, in which the thumb and the index finger touch and the remaining three fingers are upright, but slightly bent. This mudrā symbolizes prajñā (thumb) and compassion (index finger) being joined, from which the teachings flow forth for all beings (symbolized by the remaining three fingers). In the heart of Prajñāpāramitā there is a lotus with the yellow syllable MAM upright on it.

With Prajñāpāramitā in the middle being surrounded by four other figures, the whole visualization is arranged like a maṇḍala. In front of Prajñāpāramitā there is Buddha Śākyamuni sitting on a lion throne on a moon disk. In the back, on a lotus and moon disk, Avalokiteśvara sits in the cross-legged position. To the right kneels Śāriputra with his palms joined. To the left Ānanda sits on a lotus. Though Ānanda does not appear as a person in the *Heart Sūtra*, he is implicitly present and therefore included in this maṇḍala here. As mentioned above, he is the one to whom the Buddha entrusted the preservation and passing on of the prajñāpāramitā sūtras, which is indicated by Ānanada's opening words "Thus have I heard" at the beginning of the sūtra. These five figures are the cast, so to speak, of the sūtra, the main actors. Of course, the leading actress is Prajñāpāramitā in the center and she is also the all-pervading theme or story line. Once that visualization is complete, we imagine that from the syllable MAṂ in Prajñāpāramitā's heart light radiates to all buddhas and bodhisattvas (jñānasattvas, or wisdom beings), makes offerings to them, and has them melt into the five figures of the maṇḍala. The five also receive *abhiṣeka* from all buddhas, with Vairocana, Akṣobhya, Ratnasambhava, Amitābha, and Amoghasiddhi (or their corresponding syllables OṂ, HŪṂ, TRAṂ, HRĪḤ, ĀḤ) being placed on top of the heads of Prajñāpāramitā, the Buddha, Śāriputra, Avalokiteśvara, and Ānanda, respectively. In addition, all five are blessed through a white syllable OṂ at their foreheads, a red syllable ĀḤ at their throats, and a blue syllable HŪṂ at their hearts.

As usual, it is said that our visualization should be like a reflection in a mirror or a rainbow—clear, lucid, and vivid yet entirely nonsubstantial. Having focused on this maṇḍala and brought it clearly to mind, we then visualize that the Buddha moves onto a lotus in the heart of ourselves as Prajñāpāramitā and enters his samādhi. Through moving into the heart of Prajñāpāramitā, he unites with Prajñāpāramitā, since that samādhi means to rest in prajñāpāramitā. This then empowers Avalokiteśvara to answer Śāriputra's question, while Ānanda sits on his lotus. All four figures are now in the heart center of ourselves as Prajñāpāramitā.

As for what to do with our mind, that is, how to rest in samādhi during this visualization, the sādhana says:

In this way, the entire retinue which evolves from
The state of all phenomena being at peace is embodied in
   the mother.
Observe the letter MAṂ in the samādhi with characteristics
Clearly and without conceptions.

All phenomena, primordially at peace,
Appear mistakenly through the power of conditions.
When reality is realized, they are at peace.
When they are at peace, they appear like illusions.

Do not be separated from not conceptualizing them as the
   four extremes.
Without dwelling in agitation or dullness, mind as such

Is luminous, not meditating on anything—
This is the perfection of the yoga without characteristics.

Thus, we employ two types of samādhi here. The first one is to focus on the lucid yet insubstantial syllable MAṂ in the heart center of Prajñāpāramitā, with the Buddha being in samādhi and Avalokiteśvara teaching. This is the samādhi with characteristics, or with visualization. The point here is to have a sense of the visualization being the union of emptiness and appearance (or clarity). Next, we switch to the samādhi without characteristics, which means to contemplate that all phenomena are illusions, appearing yet empty of true existence. Thus, they are not existent, nonexistent, both existent and nonexistent, nor neither. Without finding any reference points whatsoever, we just rest in mind's luminous and open spaciousness without meditating on anything, free from agitation and dullness. That is, we simply let go and allow our mind to settle into its own nature as it is, without visualizing or holding on to anything. During a session we can also alternate several times between these two samādhis.

Finally, the sādhana says that, when we are tired, we recite the mantra OṂ GATE GATE PĀRAGATE PĀRASAṂGATE BODHI SVĀHĀ, which is the *Heart Sūtra* in a nutshell. Note that, different from the common practice in Tibetan Buddhism, in Indian sādhanas the mantra recitation is not used during the entire period of visualization and meditation, but only as a means of resting at the end of a session. While reciting the mantra (either silently in our mind or with a quiet voice) and keeping the visualization in mind, we visualize the syllables of the mantra surrounding the MAṂ in the heart center of ourselves as Prajñāpāramitā. We imagine that light radiates out from the syllables of the mantra to all wisdom beings (all buddhas and bodhisattvas), makes offerings to them, and returns with their blessings. Then the light radiates toward all sentient beings and purifies their minds, establishing them in the state of Prajñāpāramitā.

Finally, we recite the eighteen emptinesses and dissolve the visualization from the outside to the inside, with the syllable MAṂ dissolving last, from bottom to top.

The Sūtra of the Heart of the Glorious Lady Prajñāpāramitā

Thus have I heard. Once the Bhagavān was residing on Vulture Flock Mountain in Rājagṛha together with a great assembly of fully ordained monks and a great assembly of bodhisattvas. At that time the Bhagavān entered the samādhi of the enumerations of phenomena called "perception of the profound." At the same time noble Avalokiteśvara, the bodhisattva mahāsattva, while practicing the profound prajñāpāramitā, saw the following: he saw the five skandhas to be empty of nature.

Then, through the power of the Buddha, venerable Śāriputra spoke thus to noble Avalokiteśvara, the bodhisattva mahāsattva: "How should a son of noble family or a daughter of noble family train who wishes to practice the profound prajñāpāramitā?"

Noble Avalokiteśvara, the bodhisattva mahāsattva, said to venerable Śāriputra, "O Śāriputra, a son of noble family or a daughter of noble family who wishes to practice the profound prajñāpāramitā should see in this way: they see the five skandhas to be empty of nature. Form is emptiness; emptiness also is form. Emptiness is no other than form; form is no other than emptiness. In the same way, feeling, discrimination, formation, and consciousness are emptiness. Thus, Śāriputra, all phenomena are emptiness, without characteristics, without arising, without ceasing, without stain, not without stain, without decrease, and without increase. Therefore, Śāriputra, in emptiness there is no form, no feeling, no discrimination, no formation, no consciousness; no eye, no ear, no nose, no tongue, no body, no mind; no form, no sound, no smell, no taste, no tangible object, no phenomenon; no eye dhātu up to no mind dhātu, no dhātu of phenomena, no mental consciousness dhātu; no ignorance, no termination of ignorance up to no aging and death and no termination of aging and death; no suffering, no origin, no cessation, no path, no wisdom, no attainment, and no nonattainment.

"Therefore, Śāriputra, since bodhisattvas have no attainment, they abide by relying on prajñāpāramitā. Since their minds are without obscuration, they have no fear. Having fully transcended delusion, they attain complete nirvāṇa. All the buddhas who abide in the three times fully awaken to unsurpassable completely perfect enlightenment by relying on prajñāpāramitā.

"Therefore, the great mantra of prajñāpāramitā, the mantra of great insight, the unsurpassed mantra, the mantra equal to the unequaled, the mantra that calms all suffering, should be known to be true since it is undeceiving. The prajñāpāramitā mantra is said as follows:

OM GATE GATE PĀRAGATE PĀRASAMGATE BODHI
SVĀHĀ

"In this way, Śāriputra, bodhisattva mahāsattvas should train in the profound prajñāpāramitā."

Then the Bhagavān rose from that samādhi and spoke to noble Avalokiteśvara, the bodhisattva mahāsattva, "Well done! Good, good, O son of noble family. Thus it is, O son of noble family, thus it is. One should practice the profound prajñāpāramitā just as you have taught and the tathāgatas will rejoice."

When the Bhagavān had said this, venerable Śāriputra and noble Avalokiteśvara, the bodhisattva mahāsattva, all those surrounding them, and the world with its gods, humans, asuras, and gandharvas rejoiced and praised the words of the Bhagavān.

This was translated into Tibetan by the Indian paṇḍita Vimalamitra and the transla-tor and fully ordained monk Rinchen Dé. It was edited by the great editor-translator Gelo, Namka, and others.

English translation by Karl Brunnhölzl based on several Tibetan and Sanskrit editions.

Selected Bibliography

Bokar, Rinpoche, and Khenpo Donyo. 1994. *Profound Wisdom of the Heart Sutra and Other Teachings*. San Francisco: ClearPoint Press.

Conze, Edward, trans. 1973. *The Perfection of Wisdom in Eight Thousand Lines & Its Verse Summary*. Bolinas: Four Seasons.

——, trans. 1975. *The Large Sutra on Perfect Wisdom*. Berkeley: University of California Press.

——, trans. 2002. *Perfect Wisdom. The Short Prajñāpāramitā Texts*. (Reprint; orig. publ. 1973 by Luzac, London). Totnes (UK): Buddhist Publishing Group.

Dārika. *Prajñāpāramitāhṛdayasādhana*. Tibetan Tripiṭaka: D2641.

Hixon, Lex. 1993. *The Mother of the Buddhas*. Wheaton: Quest Books.

Lopez, Donald S., Jr. 1988. *The Heart Sūtra Explained*. Albany: State University of New York Press.

——. 1996. *Elaborations on Emptiness*. Princeton: Princeton University Press.

Red Pine. 2005. *The Heart Sutra: The Womb of Buddhas*. Berkeley: Counterpoint Press.

Sangharakshita. 1993. *Wisdom Beyond Words: The Buddhist Vision of Ultimate Reality*. Birmingham: Windhorse Publications.

Soeng, Mu. 2010. *The Heart of the Universe: Exploring the Heart Sutra*. Boston: Wisdom Publications.

Tenzin Gyatso, the Fourteenth Dalai Lama. 2005. *Essence of the Heart Sutra*. Boston: Wisdom Publications.

Thich Nhat Hanh. 1988. *The Heart of Understanding: Commentaries on the Prajñaparamita Heart Sutra*. Berkeley: Parallax Press.